THE ANARCHIST EXPROPRIATORS

Buenaventura Durruti and Argentina's
Working-Class Robin Hoods

THE ANARCHIST EXPROPRIATORS

Buenaventura Durruti and Argentina's Working-Class Robin Hoods

Osvaldo Bayer

The Anarchist Expropriators: Buenaventura Durruti and Argentina's Working-Class Robin Hoods

© Osvaldo Bayer c/o Guillermo Schavelzon & Asoc., Agencia Literaria, www.schavelzon.com.
© 2015 Paul Sharkey, translator.
This edition © 2015 AK Press (Oakland, Edinburgh, Baltimore).

ISBN: 978-1-84935-223-9
E-ISBN: 978-1-84935-224-6
Library of Congress Control Number: 2015942524

Kate Sharpley Library
BM Hurricane
London WC1N 3XX
UK
www.katesharpleylibrary.net

AK Press
674-A 23rd Street
Oakland, CA 94612
USA
www.akpress.org
akpress@akpress.org

AK Press
PO Box 12766
Edinburgh EH8 9YE
Scotland
www.akuk.com
ak@akedin.demon.co.uk

The above addresses would be delighted to provide you with the latest AK Press distribution catalog, which features books, pamphlets, zines, and stylish apparel published and/or distributed by AK Press. Alternatively, visit our websites for the complete catalog, latest news, and secure ordering.

Cover design by Josh MacPhee.
Index by John Barker.
Printed in the USA on acid-free paper.

CONTENTS

Introduction   1

Chronology of Events   15

The Anarchist Expropriators   25

Appendix: A Note on Severino Di Giovanni   135

Index   141

Introduction

It's a chastening thought that Osvaldo Bayer wrote this book nearly forty years ago and his work still challenges us, as anarchists, with ideas, arguments, and problems that are still as relevant today as they were in 1975 or, indeed, as when the actions of this narrative were originally carried out.

Much of Bayer's work belongs to the first wave of modern anarchist historiography that was, and still is, concerned with excavating anarchism's stories; research that began to challenge our ideas as to what anarchism is and had been. Some of those early pioneering works include those by James J. Martin (1953) and Voline (first English translations in 1954 and 1955) as well as the works of Antonio Tellez (1974 in English), Bill Fishman (1975), Hal Sears (1977), and Paul Avrich (1978).[1] These authors, together with Bayer and others, made the 1970s an exciting time for anarchist research. *The Anarchist Expropriators* was first published in 1975 as *Los Anarquistas Expropriados y otros ensyos* and is here published in its first English translation. It appeared shortly after what we consider to be Bayer's greatest work, the four volume *La Patagonia Rebelde* (1972–1975), soon to be published in one volume as *Rebellion in Patagonia* by AK Press. A later work, *Simon Radowitzky and the People's Justice* (1991), was recently published by Elephant Editions. Bayer and some of the other writers mentioned here were lucky enough to know some of the relatives and comrades of those who feature in their work, and this knowledge informs their narratives with a richness and immediacy that later histories often lack.

The Anarchist Expropriators is a companion piece to Bayer's earlier work *Severino Di Giovanni idealists de la violencia* (1970), which was translated into English as *Anarchism and Violence* by Elephant Editions in 1985. The main protagonist of that work,

---

1   James J. Martin, *Men Against the State* (De Kalb, IL: Adrian Allen, 1953); Voline, *The Unknown Revolution* (New York: Libertarian Bookclub, 1955); Antonio Tellez, *Sabaté: Guerilla Extraordinary* (London: Davis-Poynter, 1974); William J. Fishman, *East End Jewish Radicals, 1875–1914* (London: Duckworth, 1975); Hal Sears, *The Sex Radicals: Free Love in High Victorian America* (Lawrence: University of Kansas, 1977); Paul Avrich, *An American Anarchist: The Life of Voltairine de Cleyre* (Princeton, NJ: Princeton University Press, 1978).

Severino Di Giovanni, is glimpsed only occasionally in this volume, which in essence concentrates on other groups of anarchists carrying out acts of expropriation and revenge both alongside Di Giovanni and his comrades and after Di Giovanni's execution on February 1, 1931. It presents us with additional information on the Argentinian anarchist expropriation movement that peaked during the twenties and thirties. Vicious infighting between anarchists, ruthless state opposition, bad luck, and its own ineptness destroyed this complex, challenging, and provocative movement, and Bayer attempts to show how that happened. Like *Anarchism and Violence*, the book is short on analysis but long on action. Events hurtle along at breathtaking speed and, by the final page, we are left breathless (and a little confused as to what has just happened!).

It is best not to read this book as a portrayal of the romantic outsiders who cannot fit into society and take a principled stand against all the everyday hypocrisies they see in anarchists and the rest of the world—the Stirnerite individualists going out guns blazing, proudly proclaiming their identity in a world that constantly attempts to suffocate them. Undoubtedly there are traces of that, but the people here are a little different from Di Giovanni and others who featured in Bayer's earlier work. You won't find in these pages the heightened language, the passionate hyperbole, the tragic hero set against the world. Men such as Miguel Arcangel Roscigna and Juan Antonio Moran seem much more hardheaded and pragmatic. In different circumstances, they could have been the 1936 version of Durruti who survived his own expropriation career and, during the period covered by this volume, was no different from these men. Indeed Durruti thought so highly of Roscigna and his activities that he wanted him to come to Spain and help with the anarchist struggle there.

Argentinian anarchism in the twenties and thirties was a product of brutal state repression against a movement that, in the early part of the twentieth century, was a force to be reckoned with.[2] This repression, exemplified by the events of 1st May 1909, the Social Defense Law of 1910, and the Tragic Week of 1919, together with a constant, brutal day-to-day treatment at the hands of the police and other agencies, reflected the concern anarchism engendered in the authorities. Reacting to these and other factors, such as the popularity of syndicalism among the working class, some anarchists began to analyze and reflect on what they believed and where they thought these beliefs should take the movement. Spurred on by the events of the Russian revolution, writers such as Lopez Arango and Abad de Santillan, for instance, were teasing out the relationship between syndicalism and anarchism in the labor movement, discussing the nature of trade unions, and the intricacies of class as the "lodestar" of

---

2   See for example, Juan Suriano, trans. by Chuck Morse, *Paradoxes of Utopia: Anarchist Culture and Politics in Buenos Aires, 1890–1910* (Oakland: AK Press, 2010).

anarchism as they attempted to rebuild a movement that would bring about the world they desired. The primary vehicle for this discussion was *La Protesta*, the paper they edited.

All this is well and good, but there were still profound differences in the movement and, as is so often the case, this slice of anarchist history reverberates with internecine quarrels—quarrels that became bitter and bloody but, in themselves, are reminiscent of similar quarrels in other countries and at other times. In essence, they revolved around those constant and exhausting questions of what anarchism is and the best way to practice it and bring about anarchy. Bayer is careful to try to delineate the complexities of these differences and provides us with a useful guide to understanding them.

But there is still a little more that we may need to consider. Personality clashes and questions of ownership of resources had a deleterious effect on theory and practice. The execution of one of *La Protesta*'s editors, Lopez Arango, probably by Di Giovanni, in October 1929 is chilling. This though was not the first time that violence had occurred within Argentinian anarchism. We should remember that, in August 1924, gunmen from *La Protesta* raided the anarchist paper *Pampa Libre* leaving one dead and three wounded. These were not simply intellectual and practical differences between comrades, but ones that were visceral, deeply felt, and with deadly consequences. Such tensions brought about some kind of fractured dialectic between the realities of the world outside the movement and the antagonisms within it. The results were not edifying.

Understanding the development of these tensions is not easy from this distance. One senses that much of the antagonism on the part of those around *La Antorcha* (presented in this volume as essentially *La Protesta*'s most constant critic) who had broken away from *La Protesta* in 1921, consisted of a number of factors. A major concern was the printing press and resources that *La Protesta* owned: who gave the present editors the right to own them and why weren't these resources shared across the movement? Secondly, and just as importantly, was the fact that *La Protesta* saw itself as *THE* paper of the Argentinian anarchist movement (with the backing of the FORA) while *La Antorcha* saw itself as *ONE* of the papers of a much more diverse anarchist movement than the one with which those around *La Protesta* identified. The editors of *La Antorcha* certainly did not offer whole-hearted support to the expropriators, but it did support expropriator anarchists who were imprisoned (unlike *La Protesta* who saw them as "anarcho-bandits"). It also condemned *La Protesta*'s habit of naming or slandering those who had committed expropriations (*La Protesta*, for instance, described Di Giovanni as a "fascist agent"), calling the editors police informers. Hence the question of violence may not have been quite as central as Bayer suggests in driving the antagonism between the two papers. All this, remember, occurred between groups of people, many of whom had worked together in previous years, and indeed would in future ones.

A feature of the Argentinian movement was its internationalism. Italian, German, Spanish, and Russian anarchists regularly traveled in and out of the country, providing the movement with both a richness of ideas and strategies, as well as all the practical realities that internationalism actually meant—not so much a theory, more a way of life. The French anarchist Gaston Leval was associated with *La Antorcha*, while Abad de Santillan, one of the editors of *La Protesta*, was in Berlin between 1922 and 1926 working with the International Workingmen's Association (IWMA) as the Argentine Regional Workers' Federation (FORA) delegate, and this is reflected in the pages of the various newspapers. *La Protesta* regularly sent assistance back to Italian anarchists both before and after the rise of Italian fascism, while many articles from the strong Italian anarchist community in Argentina were aimed at those anarchists trapped in Italy or in exile, as well as attacking Italian fascists in Argentina. Meanwhile, *La Antorcha* published writings on the situation for anarchists in Russia as well as in Italy and other countries.

It should come as no surprise, then, that the struggle against fascism resonated within the Argentinian anarchist movement. The struggle against the death sentence placed on Sacco and Vanzetti was equally important and influential. Di Giovanni and others were in regular contact with the American, Italian-language paper *L'Adunata dei Refrattari* throughout the campaign and, after the executions, Sacco's companion wrote to Di Giovanni thanking him and his comrades for their efforts on behalf of the two men; efforts that had included bombings as well as other more sedate propaganda activities.

This internationalism took an interesting turn in early August 1925 with the arrival of members of the Spanish "Los Solidarios" group, who were on the run from Europe and fresh from robbing a bank in Santiago, Chile. By October 1925 they had commenced activities in Buenos Aires and, by January 1926, had help and support from Argentinian comrades there. The Los Solidarios members (Ascaso, Durruti, and Jover) were robbing banks, metro stations, and tram depots to raise funds to support revolutionary activity in Spain—and quite probably in Argentina too. During their time in the country, they became close to Roscigna and others who would be active in the fight to prevent the deportation of the three Spaniards from France to Argentina (they had left the country in spring 1926), where they were wanted for killing a policeman and a bank employee during the course of their robberies. It was a fight that *La Protesta* described as "not qualifying for the description of anarchist." It was a statement that only added to the tension between the various anarchist tendencies.

Roscigna belonged to part of the anarchist movement that insisted on maintaining what they felt was an ideological purity; there could be no joint front with communists against fascism or in support of Sacco and Vanzetti, for example. In Russia, these communists had been responsible for the murder, execution, and imprisonment of countless anarchists. To work with them in any way would betray the memory of these dead, and would dilute anarchism into some type of pragmatic convenience. How could people know what anarchism was unless it remained pure? An anarchist movement could not be built on joint and popular fronts. Rather Roscigna and others favored a sort of permanent confrontationalism, a constant war against capitalism and the state where anarchism would make no compromise. In 1924, the FORA had expelled those around *La Antorcha* and other anarchist papers from the "Comite Pro Presos y Deportados" (Prisoners and Deported Solidarity Group), and in response these papers had called for direct aid to anarchist prisoners, their families, and the families of those deported. For Roscigna and his comrades, the aim was not just getting funds to anarchist prisoners but to get them out of prison—and that would take time and money. To that end, he also became fascinated by the possibilities counterfeiting offered. In a sense his move to expropriation was a logical one, re-enforced by those from Spain who were engaged in the same strategy, who came from a similar social background as himself and possessed the moral purity he felt essential in order to describe oneself as anarchist.

Moran, the other major protagonist of Bayer's work, showed a similar pragmatism. Twice General Secretary of the powerful Maritime Workers

Federation, Moran fought a constant running battle against scab labor and intimidation. It was a battle he felt could not be won by conventional means, and he was part of the group who decided to execute Major Rosasco, the man spearheading attacks on anarchists, labor radicals, and others. The statement of those who carried out the execution ended with the words "these proletarian fighters have shown, by executing Rosasco, how we may be rid of the dictatorship, root and branch." Like the Spanish action groups, Moran shared the belief that, sometimes, extreme measures were the only defense available to unions and organizations. One had to fight fire with fire or be destroyed.

Of course it is never that simple, never that straightforward. It's easy for us to create patterns that were not there or lose sight of the nuances that have become hidden over the years. We can't be certain why people do what they do or how events around them shaped their actions. We can say, though, to see the necessity of using arms to obtain funds does not necessarily mean that those who arrived at this position were any good at it in practice. Los Solidarios gained hardly any money from some of their efforts, while the Spanish anarchist group around Pere Boadas—a member of "The Nameless Ones" and not Los Solidarios as Bayer suggests—were murderously inept in their raid on the Messina Bureau de Change at the Plaza de la Independence on the afternoon of October 25th, 1928. Their arrest led to other raids being undertaken to fund their escape (which succeeded) and, eventually, their actions would lead to more arrests.

As time went on, more of the groups were arrested, which resulted in more energy spent on working out how to free the imprisoned comrades. The groups began to live in a world of their own—always a danger in work of this sort, and especially so as the popular support base erodes. As part of his everyday work, Moran may have been able to chat with people who weren't taking part in actions and, by doing so, he was able to temper his actions with realism. It became harder for others who, perhaps, grew more contemptuous of those who did not share their commitment and found it hard to know who to trust. The movement, if that is what it was, became more and more concerned with revenge on individual policemen as their comrades were killed and imprisoned. It became a small world of attack and counter attack with the protagonists known to each other, and everyone else relegated to onlookers. For the members of Los Solidarios there was always the organization in Spain; for the Argentinian anarchist expropriators there eventually was just themselves.

Of course the tension with the various strands in the anarchist movement increased as the actions continued and state repression grew worse. None of the tendencies appeared to understand the position of the others. Indeed one senses that they were determined not to! For those around *La Protesta* the most important work that anarchists could do was to create a movement; to bring numbers of the working class and others to their cause; to hold meetings, talk to people, produce newspapers, and pamphlets that would build an educated, mass movement that could sweep the dirt of capitalism away. In their opinion, those in the action groups actively prevented this from happening. They put anarchism on the defensive, created a false impression of what anarchism was, and alienated everyone. If they did that, if they prevented the movement's growth, they were, objectively, assets of the state.

Looking at it now from the hindsight of ninety or so years it all becomes horribly poignant. There seems to be no common ground between the antagonists and, yet again, anarchist history gets bogged down in its own quarrels and vendettas. However we read and interpret Bayer's work, it is a challenge to discover anything positive. Thoughtful attempts to define the ideas of anarchism and its possibilities as carried out by Santillan etc. on one hand, versus a frustration with theory and a logical move to expropriation, often characterized by exemplary bravery and courage, on the other.

Yet there are matters that should concern us here. The ending is unbearable with the murder of Moran and the others. Just as painful, if not more so, is the escape attempt of the anarchist prisoners in Caseros. With no hope of outside help, essentially abandoned, they still made their attempt. Expropriators some of them may have been, but to abandon them? Surely no "correct" anarchist line is worth the abandonment of those who also profess anarchism. We may have the right answer (even if we haven't the mass movement to celebrate the fact) but comradeship, in anarchism, has to sometimes cross the boundaries between those who agree with every word you say and those who question your methods and practices in the most profound way possible. As a comrade in *La Antorcha* wrote, "the expropriators were always better than those who repressed them" and it appears that some forgot this.

Some of the survivors of this story appear again in Spain during the revolution. Some played important roles, others less so. All were fighting fascism and attempting to create the most profound revolution we have, so far, known. Abad de Santillan was working hand-in-hand with Spanish anarchists who had been members of action groups and, at times, expropriators. Circumstances change and, when you think you are winning, all is forgiven. As we said earlier, the qualities of a Roscigna, or a Moran, could have blossomed in Barcelona before the May Days of 1937 and if we want to admire a Durruti or Ascaso for how they made their lives ("mistakes" and all) in trying to help construct a new world, perhaps the anarchist expropriators are worthy of a similar respect. Let's see where that takes us.

—Kate Sharpley Library

Chronology of Events

June 18, 1897.
The first issue of *La Protesta Humana* is published. In 1903 it becomes *La Protesta*.

March 25–26, 1901.
FOA (Argentine Workers Federation) is formed with approximately ten thousand members. It is syndicalist in nature and rejects party political involvement.

1905.
At its Fifth Congress, FOA becomes the FORA (Argentine Regional Workers' Federation) with a commitment to anarchist communism.

May 1, 1909.
A cavalry detachment under the overall command of Ramon Falcon, Chief of Police, opens fire on a demonstration in Plaza Lorea. Several demonstrators are killed and many wounded. An ensuing General strike last nine days with over two-thousand arrests.

November 13, 1909.
Eighteen-year-old Ukrainian anarchist Simon Radowitzky throws a bomb at Falcon's car, killing both Falcon and Falcon's secretary. Due to his age, he will be sentenced to indefinite imprisonment.

Martial law is declared and remains until January 1910. The offices and printing press of *La Protesta* are destroyed during this period.

April, 1915.
9th Congress of FORA reverses their support for anarchist communism. A minority of members break away and form FORA V, remaining committed to anarchist communism. This is the FORA that appears in this book. The majority become FORA 1X.

December, 1918.
A strike breaks out at the Vasena metal works in Buenos Aires.

January 2–14, 1919.
Events take place that will become known as *La Semana Trajica* (The Tragic Week).

January 7, 1919.
Strikers attempted to stop a shipment of materials from leaving the plant. The police open fire, killing five workers and wounding many.

January 9, 1919.
Violence breaks out between police and mourners at the funeral of the five workers killed outside the Vasena plant. The two FORAs call for a General Strike.

January 10, 1919 onwards.
The right-wing Argentine Patriotic League attack the Russian Jewish areas of Buenos Aires.

January 12, 1919.
The 9th Congress FORA decide to call off the General Strike.

January 14, 1919.
Police raid the offices of *La Protesta* and smash its printing press.

January 20, 1919.
The strike is called off. Over the course of the Tragic Week, fifty thousand would be imprisoned and many workers killed.

May 19, 1919.
The first politically motivated armed robbery in Argentina takes place as the manager of a bureau de change

is targeted. It is a failure with no money taken and a policeman killed. The robbers are captured.

1921.

The newspaper *La Antorcha* breaks away from *La Protesta* and will run until 1932.

1920–1922.

A series of strikes, general strikes, and insurrections take place among the rural workers of Patagonia. In 1921, hundreds of striking workers (some of whom had surrendered) were summarily executed by the 10th Cavalry under the command of Colonel Hector Varela.

January 27, 1923.

Colonel Hector Varela is killed by the Tolstoyan anarchist Kurt Wilckens in response to the killings of workers in Patagonia.

June 16, 1923.

Kurt Wilckens is murdered in prison by a member of the right-wing Patriotic League, aided by the connivance of prison officials.

August 4, 1924.

Gunmen from *La Protesta* and FORA wreck the presses of anarchist newspaper *Pampa Libre*. One person is killed, several are injured.

September, 1924.

FORA advises its members to boycott the anarchist newspaper *La Antorcha*.

June 9, 1925.

Three members of the Spanish action group Los Solidarios (Ascaso, Durruti, and Jover) arrive in Valparaiso, Chile.

July 11, 1925.

Los Solidarios rob the Bank of Chile in Santiago

Early August 1925.

The group moves on to Buenos Aires.

August 1925.

C*ulmine*, the paper of Di Giovanni and the Renzo Novatore group, appears as a monthly journal.

October 18, 1925.

An armed raid by Los Solidarios on Las Meras tram depot nets very little money.

November 17, 1925.

Los Solidarios raid on Primera Junta metro station results in the death of a policeman and little money taken.

January 19, 1926.

Roscigna and others are involved in the robbery of a provincial bank in San Martin. Substantial money is taken with one employee killed and one wounded.

February 1926–April 1928.
Culmine appears as a weekly.

April 30, 1926.
Ascaso and Durruti arrive in France. Jover arrives soon after them.

December 1926.
Of the protests and campaign to resist the extradition of Ascaso, Durruti, and Jover from France to Argentina, *La Protesta* writes "they do not qualify for the description anarchist."

April, 1927.
Extradition of Ascaso, Durruti, and Jover from France to Argentina is confirmed.

July, 1927.
The time limit for extradition runs out and Ascaso, Durruti, and Jover are released in Paris and immediately extradited to Belgium.

October 1, 1927.
Raid on Rawson Hospital is coordinated by Roscigna to gain funds for anarchist prisoners. A policeman is killed during the raid and Roscigna and others flee to Uruguay. The proceeds from the raid are used to make counterfeit money.

August 11–16, 1928.
Tenth Congress of FORA is held—the last major congress of the federation for fifty years.

October 20, 1928.
Pere Boadas, a member of the Spanish action group The Nameless Ones leads a raid on a bureau de change in the Cambio Messina in Montivideo. Boadas had been sent to Argentina to encourage Roscigna to come to Spain and work with the anarchists there. The raid is carried out against Roscigna's advice, and three people are killed (a business man, a shoeshine boy, and a taxi driver).

November 9, 1928.
Boadas and others are arrested.

May 20, 1929.
FORA stages a twenty-four-hour strike in solidarity with the "Free Radowitzky" campaign.

October 25, 1929.
Someone (Di Giovanni?) assassinates Emilio Lopez Arango, an editor of *La Protesta*.

April 13, 1930.
Radowitzky reprieved and expelled to Uruguay.

October 2, 1930.
Roscigna and Di Giovanni rob a sanitary services wage clerk, taking 286,000 pesos. The money is used to fund

the escape of Boadas et al. in March the following year.

January 29, 1931.
Di Giovanni and Scarfo are arrested.

February 1, 1931.
Di Giovanni is executed by firing squad.

February 2, 1931.
Paulino Scarfo is executed by firing squad.

March 18, 1931.
In an escape plan engineered by Roscigna and Gino Gatti, an Italian anarchist, Boadas and three others from the Cambio Messina raid are sprung from prison through as carefully constructed tunnel. Three anarchist members of the Bakers Union also are freed.

March 27, 1931.
Roscigna and others are arrested.

June 12, 1931.
Juan Antonio Moran and others shoot and kill Major Rosasco in retaliation for his ill treatment of prisoners, including the use of torture.

July 11, 1931.
Pere Boadas is arrested. He is released in 1953.

September 6, 1931.
The era of military government begins. The worker's movement is attacked, newspapers are shut down, and trade unions and political and cultural organizations are banned. Anarchists are imprisoned or deported.

Sept 1932.
Martial law is lifted. *La Antorcha* and *La Protesta* and various unions bring out the joint manifesto *Eighteen Months of Military Terror*.

June 28, 1933.
Juan Antonio Moran is captured.

August 11, 1933.
Juan del Piano, the last of the expropriators at large, is killed by the police.

October 7, 1933.
Anarchist prisoners in Caseros make an escape attempt. It fails. Three guards and one anarchist are killed.

May 10, 1935.
Juan Antonio Moran is released for lack of evidence, and is kidnapped outside the prison.

May 12, 1935.
Juan Antonio Moran's body is found. He had been shot in the head.

December 31, 1936.
Miguel Arcangel Roscigna and three others are released from prison in Uruguay, and handed over to the Argentinian police. Roscigna and two others disappear while in police custody. Their bodies are never recovered.

—Kate Sharpley Library

The Anarchist Expropriators

Opposed, vilified, even by other libertarian currents, the anarchist "expropriator" movement, as its supporters described themselves—otherwise, illegalist anarchism—was in vogue in Argentina in the 1920s and 1930s.

Recollecting and writing their story is certainly not the same as claiming it for one's own. Offering an objective explanation of how society developed just three or four decades ago is not just a difficult undertaking but, above all, it's a risky one. Precisely because of the confusion between objectivity and partisanship.

Who, for example, would question the tale of Robin Hood, which every child has read? Now Robin

Hood took from the rich and gave to the poor—and "taking," robbing, and expropriating are all synonyms. But at several centuries' distance, Robin Hood looks like an attractive personality, maybe because his life is the stuff of legend, or because it is merely the product of the imagination. But the anarchist expropriators are not products of the imagination. They existed—and how! Not that they were all Robin Hoods, any more than they were all Scarlet Pimpernels.[1] They were intractable when it came to defending their lives, because they knew that one false move or the slightest sign of weakness meant they would be executed in the street or in front of a firing squad. In a way, they were urban guerrillas, but they could not rely on any foreign power for funds and weapons, and there was nowhere to seek asylum when things got too hot. They lived from day to day, without any breaks. They were interesting figures who attacked society ("bourgeois" society) with bombs and revolvers, while their newspapers were violent in their criticism of the Bolshevik dictatorship, invoking the name of the gleaming, immanent Golden Fleece: Freedom.

"We cannot own them as ours," we were told by one of the last great anarchist intellectuals, Diego Abad de Santillán. True, but we cannot ignore them either. In Argentina, the anarchist expropriator movement

---

1   The Scarlet Pimpernel, Sir Percy Blakeney, the central character of Baroness Orczy's novel of the same name, was undaunted by enormous odds, able to infiltrate anywhere, utterly fearless, unselfish and prompted by feelings of solidarity.

was very significant—even more so, perhaps, than in Spain—even though it survived for only fifteen years. It embraced a motley crew of academics, workers, and a few outright criminals who made up a very distinct rogues' gallery.

The first politically motivated armed robbery in Argentina took place on May 19, 1919. Given the time and the setting, only Russians could have been behind it. (Society was living through the whirlwind of the Maximalist revolution in Petrograd and Moscow.) The Argentinian anarchists' ranks included a numbers of Slavs, whose names echoed through the gunfire outside trade union premises or after bomb outrages. Radowitzky, Karaschin, and Romanoff had disturbed the blithe existence of the *porteños*.[2] So whenever the newspapers named the perpetrators of this first political outrage, their readership must have nodded and exclaimed: How could it have been otherwise? It could only have been Russians!

Everything about that first outrage was singular, starting with its protagonists. This simple narrative cannot convey the atmosphere of conspiracy, the nihilistic mysticism and religious embracing of a destiny of suffering, which awaited the two political desperadoes when they shattered the tranquility of the Chacarita district with their gunfire in the late afternoon in May 1919. These were characters worthy of a Dostoyevsky novel or maybe the melancholy ironies of Chekhov.

---

2   *Porteños* are residents of Buenos Aires.

The outrage—a sign of the times this—began on a tram. Fear reigned in Buenos Aires. President Hipólito Yrigoyen[3] had lost control of the situation over recent weeks and it had all culminated in the massacre at the Vasena workshops, and the proletariat had not forgiven that.[4] El Peludo[5] was to be confronted by 367 strikes that year—two more strikes that the year has days. And while anarchist intellectuals kept arguing with one another about the society of the future, when there would be no more governments, the anarcho-individualists were bent on direct action and burning trams or blowing up bakeries.

By that point, the left had already experienced one split that had repercussions upon trade union life in Argentina: one strand of anarchism had gone over to the Russian revolution, which is to say, to the Maximalists (Bolsheviks). The other strand though, the majority anarcho-communist strand, was as critical of

3   Yrigoyen, leader of the UCR (Radical Civic Union) party, was the first president elected in Argentina by universal, secret ballot, serving between 1916 and 1922. He was re-elected in 1928, but his second term ended with General Uriburu's coup d'etat in 1930.
4   Pedro Vasena & Sons had a steelworks in Buenos Aires with a workforce of two thousand. In December, the workers struck for better pay and conditions. Police attacked their demonstration on January 7, 1919, killing a number of them. After their funerals were also attacked, a general strike was called, street fighting erupted, barricades were erected, and the military intervened. Ultra-nationalists seized the chance to mount a pogrom against Jews and immigrants, and, for a week, (Tragic Week as it was thereafter known) the city was in turmoil. The result was seven hundred dead, hundreds injured, and tens of thousands arrested.
5   *El Peludo* (armadillo) was Hipólito Yrigoyen's nickname.

capitalism as of Lenin's government, having the view that these were two forms of the same phenomenon of dictatorship.

The arguments between the two were vitriolic. The more "pragmatic" anarchists—who backed the Russian revolution—argued their case in the columns of *Bandera Roja*, while the die-hard anarcho-communists damned them as opportunists and traitors in *La Protesta*, *El Libertario*, and *Tribuna Proletaria*.

The two protagonists of the May 1919 outrage were drawn from the ranks of the anarchist faction that supported the Russian revolution. These were no "opportunists," merely Russians who sought to finance the launch of a Russian-language newspaper as a way to explain to their countrymen, who had also settled in Argentina, just what was happening in distant "mother" Russia.

The Perazzos were a couple who were doing quite nicely, thank you. They had a currency exchange at 347 Rivadavia Street, in the building that had formerly housed the Chamber of Commerce. They closed the exchange at 7:00pm every day, and went home to the Chacarita district on the No. 13 tram, which they caught in the city center and which dropped them off just a few meters from their home. Pedro A. Perazzo normally carried a briefcase.

For a few days early in May, Señora Perazzo noticed the unusual eyes of two strangers watching her through the exchange's plate glass window. One of the men was quite fair-haired with a Polish look to him, whereas the other one's eyes were dark and twinkling. She brought this to her husband's attention but he dismissed it as of no consequence. On May 19, the Perazzos left the bureau at 7:30pm, and caught the usual No. 13 tram homeward. Señor Perazzo had his briefcase with him.

En route, his wife felt unsettled; she was sure that the passenger sitting behind them was the Polish-looking stranger who had been watching incessantly lately. She told her husband, who reassured her but was actually also on the alert, for he had noticed something: the tram was being tailed by a car that had drawn up close behind several times, and one of the passengers had been sneaking a look in their direction.

As they arrived at their stop, Perazzo was more at ease. There, at the junction of Jorge Newbery and Lemos streets, there was plenty of light and traffic. Two tram routes passed that way and only fifty meters separated them from busy Triunvirato Street.

Just as he was climbing down from the tram, his wife suddenly tugged at his jacket sleeve and froze. The "Pole" had disembarked too. The tram carried on along its route. The mysterious car drew to a halt and the dark-eyed man got out.

Next the "Pole" produced a revolver and hurled himself on Perazzo, while his wife fled, screaming. Perazzo was so stunned that he clung to his briefcase. The "Pole" tried to wrest it from his grip but when that failed, he lost his cool and started shooting all over the place.

At that point, the No. 87 tram arrived on the

scene, with two policemen on the platform. Seeing the scene in front of them and hearing the gunshots, the policemen drew their guns and took aim at the car and at the fair-haired man who had finally managed to get the briefcase.

His accomplice in the car called to him, but he didn't hear and was so on edge that he ran off on foot while continuing to shoot in every direction. One bullet struck the tram-driver in the chest and he slumped to the floor.[6] Another bullet hit one of the policemen in the foot.

Unable to help their comrade, the dark-eyed man and the driver of the mystery car made their escape. The gunman, with the other policeman in pursuit, raced down Lemos Street, and then turned north down the unasphalted, pitch dark Leones Street. He reached Fraga Street, but he was jinxed: no. 225 Fraga Street was the home of two policemen, who, having heard gunfire, had come out with their guns. Spotting the malefactor—who had dumped the briefcase on the corner—they took cover behind some trees and emptied their weapons in his direction. One of their bullets shattered his left arm. Infuriated, he advanced towards the policeman hiding behind the tree, fired one lethal shot into his chest—his last bullet—and took shelter in a coal depot. The coalman, whom curiosity had

---

6   He emerged uninjured, and later told reporters that he owed his life to his two fleece-lined undershirts. After ricocheting off the floor, the bullet passed through his jacket and his first undershirt, but never penetrated the one underneath.

drawn out on to the street for a closer look, was struck in the eye by one of the policemen's bullets.

Out of ammunition and wounded, the malefactor took cover behind some flowerpots and ferns. There, he collapsed from exhaustion and was arrested.

It had all gone wrong: a real "farce." One policeman dead, the coalman and the malefactor both seriously wounded—and the latter bleeding profusely—and the Perazzos and another policeman slightly injured. All for nothing.

Who were the malefactors? That was something that would surprise the police in the course of their enquiries, which would be slow and complicated, in spite of the vengeful zeal invested in them.

The unknown offender was treated before being subjected to questioning, which must not, of course, have been unduly gentle. He was tall, beefy, pale-complexioned, with short chestnut-brown hair and Slavic features. His clothing was modest but clean. He had papers in the name of Juan Konovesuk, born in (Russian) Bessarabia on January 27, 1883. Later his real name came to light: he was Andrei Babby, a White Russian naturalized Austrian, born in Bukovina on the border of the two empires. He was thirty years old and had been a resident of Argentina for the past six years. He was a bookkeeper.

In spite of hour after hour of questioning, the police could get nothing out of him except a far-fetched story. Babby told how he had been sitting on a bench in a square, jobless, when a sinister-looking, bushy-mustached individual, known as "José the German," had invited him to have lunch with him and offered him a "simple job" that paid a few pesos. All he had to do was follow a couple (the Perazzos) on the tram and snatch a briefcase from the man when they got off. Babby said that he was afraid to refuse and that, once on board the tram, he had seen "José the German" following in a car and looking menacingly at him in order to make sure he did his part. Babby claimed that this was all the information he could give about this mystery man.

Each day, the *porteños* read the reports of the attack and about the investigation's progress. The newspapers carried lengthy reports on Babby's statements, and indulged themselves in speculation about "José the German." So much so that a sort of psychosis developed, wherein everybody thought they knew someone who looked that suspicious. Because of this, the police received dozens of denunciations, emanating mostly from prostitutes and café owners.

Unconvinced by Babby's story, the police conducted enquiries in all the German restaurants. But the owners and waiters were quite embarrassed about their answers, because their German clientele included lots of men who actually wore a mustache like the Kaiser's—although Wilhelm II had by then lost the war and his throne—and fitted the description.

The police received an anonymous tip about Andrei Babby's address; he had a room at 1970 Corrientes Street. On being questioned, the concierge stated that Babby shared it with a certain teacher, one Germán Boris Wladimirovich. The police asked to speak to him, but he had packed his bags on May 19.

The room was searched. From a photograph, Señora Perazzo identified Boris Wladimirovich as the dark-eyed man who had been watching her through the exchange's window and who got out of the car when Babby had snatched the briefcase from her husband.

The police, sensing that Boris Wladimirovich was the brains of the operation, jumped into action. They asked about his associates, and came up with the Caplán brothers, who readily admitted that they knew him. They said that he and Babby were anarchists and that Wladimirovich was very friendly with a member of staff at the La Plata astronomical observatory, where he was wont to visit, being an enthusiastic student of the stars.

At the observatory there was a real find: two of Boris Wladimirovich's suitcases filled with anarchist publications, books, letters, and essays. Boris's friend on the staff, who had no idea of what his friend had been mixed up in, told detectives that he did not know where Boris was, but that a Ukrainian from Berisso— one Juan Matrichenko—might be able to help them there. The police traced Matrichenko and intimated to him how worried they had been because, they claimed, they feared that Boris had been kidnapped. The quick-witted Matrichenko quickly reassured them, stating that he had recommended Boris to a friend in San Ignacio in Misiones province. Moreover, driver Luis Chelli had to know the date when he set off because Wladimirovich was always calling upon his services. Two birds with one stone! After searching the driver's home, detectives telegraphed their information to the police in Posadas. They discovered anarchist materials in Chelli's room and the Perazzos identified Chelli as the driver of the vehicle involved in the attack. It was all becoming clear now.

Wladimirovich was arrested in San Ignacio. The police found it odd that a man such as him should have turned to crime. He had the air of an academic, an intellectual about him: affable manners, an intelligent look in his eye, a face marked by a sort of inner suffering. His capture caused such a sensation that the governor of Misiones, Doctor Barreiro no less, had himself driven to the police station and spent hours conversing with the anarchist. And when the police contingent arrived from Buenos Aires, headed by Inspector Foppiano, the governor himself decided to make the long train journey to bring the prisoner back to the capital.

Before they set out, the police and provincial authorities had themselves photographed for posterity. They all sat in unnatural poses in front of Boris Wladimirovich. The Nietzschean-looking prisoner looks as if he has nothing to do with all this rigmarole, while the eminent officials are staring stiffly at the camera.

Meanwhile, police had checked out Wladimirovich's identity. He was a forty-three-year-old Russian widower and writer. *La Prensa* had additional details for its readership: "Boris Wladimirovich has an interesting personality. He is a doctor, biologist, painter, and had a certain profile among Russia's progressives. According to police files, he is alleged to be Montenegrin and a draughtsman, but he is in fact Russian and descended from a family of the nobility." At the age of twenty-nine, Boris had renounced his inheritance in order to marry a revolutionary working woman. It was known that he had squandered his personal fortune in pursuit of his ideals.

He was a doctor and biologist but had never practiced, except for a brief period as a teacher in Zurich, Switzerland. Doctor Barreiro had been able to savor a few of his scientific theses while they were traveling companions.

Boris had been a Social Democrat and had taken part in the socialist Congress in Geneva in 1904 as a Russian delegate. It was there that he had his first falling-out with Lenin, although he admired the man's intellect. As for Trotsky's positions, he preferred not to comment.

The police pressed ahead with their inquiries: Boris was the author of a number of published works, including three sociological treatises. He spoke German perfectly as well as French and Russian, and had a command of most of the tongues and dialects in use in his mother country. And he spoke Spanish relatively well. His hobby was painting: indeed he had left twenty-four canvasses behind in Buenos Aires, one of them a self-portrait. Finally, he had given lectures on anarchism in Berisso, Zárate, and in the capital.

But why had this man, an active member of the European revolutionary movement, come to Argentina?

Little by little, more details emerged. His wife's death and the awful failure of the 1905 Russian revolution had destroyed his morale. Melancholy by nature, he sought consolation in vodka, a drink that he had had a fondness for since a heart attack. He had given his home in Geneva to his co-religionists and had moved to Paris, where he decided to go on a long journey in search of rest and to recuperate from his depression. One of his friends, whose brother had some property in Santa Fe province, urged him to spend some time in Argentina. Wladimirovich arrived in 1909 and frequented Russian labor circles. After some time staying with his friend's brother, he moved to Chaco, where he spent four and a half years. He lived on what little money he had left and devoted himself to studying the region, roving from Paraná to Santiago del Estero, and exploring the Patiño marshes in particular. He lived frugally, although his taste for vodka had become more and more pronounced. In Tucumán, he had learned the news of the First World War's having erupted and had decided to return to Buenos Aires. The official mouthpiece of the Patriotic League *La Razón* stated: "he was received with open arms in Buenos Aires by the progressives who, in spite of his lengthy absence, could not forget his libertarian activity on behalf of his mother country. Indeed that very absence added to his prestige. He resumed his propaganda, giving lectures, and expounding upon his ideas with conviction before workers' circles. He would mount the rostrum, and the size of his audience scarcely mattered to him. When the riots erupted in 1919, Boris traveled down to La Chacarita to set up a revolutionary committee with a solid basis, but he came upon a gang of people who refused to abide by any program or who were incapable of doing so: all they were fit for was lashing out blindly. He was tremendously disheartened."

After the Tragic Week, Boris focused on the danger constituted by Carlés's young disciples who were threatening to kill "all Russians." In fact, "Hunt down the Russian" was a catch-phrase of those younger members of the upper and middle bourgeoisie in Buenos Aires, who had enlisted either in the Civic Guard or in the Argentine Patriotic League. During the week of bloodshed that January, they also carried out iniquitous and criminal outrages in the Jewish districts, because a Jewish person is often referred to as "the Russian" in Argentina. A few hotheads, carried away by what they believed was some sort of divine mandate, even went so far as to urge a "massacre of Russians."

Boris thought his ideas through. It was, he thought, his duty to enlighten his countrymen who had settled in Argentina, particularly with regard to the implications of the October revolution, which, he argued, would usher in undiluted human freedom. Because of that, he became truly obsessed with the notion of publishing a newspaper. He regarded it as essential that he have a newspaper at his disposal because, as some journalists reported a few weeks later (after he was released from isolation), "Those who leave Russia for Argentina are the dregs of the people, above all the Jews, who, taken all in all, represent an incoherent mass incapable of establishing a serious revolutionary program, much less putting a grand theory into practice."

But it takes money to launch a newspaper, and there were only two possible options: either organize a venture of some consequence, or, more modestly, depend upon the meager involvement of workers of Russian origin and an intellectual who would go without food for a few days in order to save money towards the printing costs of the first issue.

Given his background, Boris was not used to small beer and subsistence living. He lived from day to day, getting money from the sale of some painting or from language lessons, and did not hesitate to treat himself to a fancy restaurant meal when he was flush with money. Thus he frequented the "Marina Keller," a German restaurant on 25 de Mayo Street, where the prevailing atmosphere was quintessentially European and where there was genuine Russian vodka to be had. Boris revealed his plans to the Chelli, an anarchist driver who often left him at home in his room when the vodka had robbed him of any sense of direction. Chelli was a man of action who had also taken part in the week of strikes in January. It was Chelli who had all the information about the Perazzos.

Wladimirovich could also call upon Babby, his roommate, an anarchist whose admiration for him was such that he stood ready to sacrifice his very life for his *maestro*.

Interrogated by a police team from Posadas, Wladimirovich admitted to being the instigator and sole author of the attack. When the police allowed him to talk to Babby, he told his confederate to drop the story about "José the German" because he had already confessed.

Quite unintentionally, Boris posed a legal problem.[7] His case proved so interesting that, while he was being held in isolation, the Interior Minister and several parliamentary supporters of Yrigoyen eager to get to know him better visited him. As the minister left the prison, he told the media that "the prisoner responded with serenity to the many questions put to him." All of which left the investigating magistrate seething with indignation. He was against the high-ranking official and the deputies' visit, and raised objections, reminding them that the accused was being held in isolation and therefore denied visitors.

Argentine judges at the time were particularly severe with anarchists and with simple strikers. For example, one employee of the Gath and Chaves

---

7   There were questions over whether a prisoner should have been receiving the "visitors" that he did. The (probably conservative) magistrate was trying to unearth a conspiracy and may well have had his own suspicions about "hidden hands" (possibly Radical hands) at work behind Boris.

company was sentenced to two years in prison for having issued a call for a strike outside a store. Workers were sentenced to eight and ten years in prison for thumping a scab. And they weren't sent to some sort of ladies' finishing school: the shadow of penal servitude in Ushuaia hung over any who departed from society's prescribed norms. Although he was the president, Hipólito Yrigoyen never meddled with the internal regimen of institutions, which thus enjoyed utter impunity: this was as true of the army (as evident in the Tragic Week), as of the police (in their hinting at subversion), and the Argentine Patriotic League (a particularly thuggish para-military organization ardent in its defense of the rights of property (and run by Manuel Carlés, Admiral Domecq García, and doctors Mariano Gabastou and Alfredo Grondona), operating as a de facto defensive/offensive organization.

So we can imagine the fate that awaited the failed expropriators. Especially Babby, the cop-killer. The Jockey Club wasted no time in launching a subscription for the family of "the police victim of an anti-Argentinian gang," and raised 2,010 pesos on the very first day. (This was 1919, remember!)

La Razón challenged Wladimirovich's story about the money from the attack being destined to finance a newspaper. According to *La Razón*, his aim had been to buy the materials for bomb making. For its part, *Crítica* described them as bandits reminiscent of the "Bonnot gang," the French anarchists who attacked banks in France and Belgium at the turn of the century.

Before the court, the prosecuting counsel, Doctor Costa, asked for the death penalty for Babby, fifteen years for Wladimirovich, and two years for Chelli.

After the convicts had spent many a long month in solitary confinement in La Penitenciaria,[8] the judge, Martínez, reduced Babby's sentence to twenty-five years in prison, Wladimirovich's to ten years, and Chelli's to one year. On appeal, the prosecution asked that the original sentences be reinstated, but the judges, taking things even further, passed death sentences not just on Babby but on Wladimirovich as well.

This sentencing was hotly debated. The anarchist newspapers stated that this was a case of "class vengeance" on the part of the bench. Legal circles were shocked by the sentences: Babby's was regarded as fair in that he had fired at police officers and killed one of them, but Wladimirovich had not used any weapons. Based on what he said, this was the line taken by the trial judge: "Every criminal must answer before the court for his misdeeds and their consequences. This is why Wladimirovich cannot be charged with acts for which Babby bears the responsibility—the killing of officer Santillán and the wounding of officer Varela—insofar as there was neither connivance between them nor any complicity on the part of Boris Wladimirovich."

By contrast, the appeal court put forward the following argument: "The court would like to point

---

8   The Penitenciaria Nacional was on Las Heras Avenue in Buenos Aires. It was finally demolished in 1962.

out that the accused fostered a conspiracy, a criminal association punishable under Article 25 of the Penal Code. Although not a direct participant in the murder of Officer Santillán, Boris Wladimirovich shares in the responsibility for it, for the law's view is that there is implicit solidarity in the crimes of conspirators and it deals likewise with accomplices and perpetrators." As for the reduction of the "sentence requested by the prosecutor, the court would like to point out that the application of the law falls within its remit, both in cases where the accused presents an appeal and in those where the prosecution decides against that, and thus in no instance may the court's powers be restricted." Ricardo Seeber, Daniel J. Frías, Sotero F. Vázquez, Octavio González Roura, and Francisco Ramos Mejía endorsed the sentences, but two appeal court judges, Eduardo Newton and Jorge H. Frías, dissented and voted to confirm the court's original sentencing. It was this discord that enabled Babby and Boris to cheat death, because the court was obliged to declare that: "Given that it may not impose the death penalty upon the accused, insofar as Article 11 of the Code of Criminal Procedure requires unanimity of the court, the court sentences Andrei Babby and Boris Wladimirovich to life imprisonment."

When Boris was told his sentence, he remarked, without the slightest affectation: "The life of a propagandist of ideas such as myself is at the mercy of such contingencies. Now and in the future. I am well aware that I shall not see my ideas succeed, but others will sooner or later take up the baton."

But the life of the erstwhile biology teacher from Geneva did not include any provision for a future. A few months later he was deported to remote Ushuaia, hand-cuffed with a squad of common criminal prisoners. Though he had risked banishment to Siberia in the past, it probably never occurred to him that he might some day wind up in such a desolate region, such a ghastly penitentiary, and in such a distant land.

In prison, his health, which hadn't been good to begin with, deteriorated rapidly. His end was near, and it was hastened by poor food, cold, and the beatings that were the daily fare of those dark days in the penitentiary. Despite this, people who met Boris in Ushuaia reported that he continued to peddle his ideas among the inmates, and before he died he instigated a feat that brought his strange face back to the newspapers (*La Razón* described his appearance as "queer, sinister, and Gothic"). He was the "brains" behind the anarchists' revenge on Pérez Millán, a Patriotic League member who had killed Kurt Wilckens in a bloody incident after the killing of 1,500 in Patagonia.[9] For his own protection and in order to spare him from the sentence such an offence would have merited, Pérez Millán was

---

9   Wilckens had assassinated Colonel Varela whom anarchists held accountable for the execution of 1,500 workers and *peons* in Patagonia. Thrown into prison, Wilckens in turn was murdered in his sleep by the nationalist Pérez Millán, a friend of Dr. Carlés, the president of the Argentine Patriotic League.

passed off as insane and was sent to the insane asylum in Vieytes Street. Revolted by Wilckens's killing and having discovered that Pérez Millán had been committed as insane to the Vieytes asylum, Boris Wladimirovich set about faking a nervous breakdown of his own, degenerating into complete madness in Ushuaia. He knew that mental cases from Ushuaia were transferred to the criminal cells in the Vieytes asylum, and contrived to ensure that this was the case with himself. Once he'd arrived at the Vieytes asylum, however, he was taken to a different wing from Pérez Millán, who enjoyed privileged treatment in a special little wing. Thanks to the Buenos Aires anarchists, Boris got hold of a revolver and passed it to Lucich, an inmate who enjoyed free access to all areas. With his powers of persuasion, Boris convinced Lucich to avenge Wilckens by killing Pérez Millán, which Lucich duly did. For the anarchists, this revenge was a question of honor—so much so that those in the know about Boris's part in Pérez Millán's death hailed the one-time Russian aristocrat as a hero of their movement.

Boris's involvement triggered further maltreatment, which quickly brought about his death. In his later years, both of Boris's legs were paralyzed, and he had to crawl if he wanted to leave his cell: a character from Dostoyevsky who met a Dostoyevskian end, like someone out of *The Insulted and Humiliated* or *The House of the Dead*.

This singular initial eruption of expropriator anarchism in Argentina triggered a long debate that lingered through the entire period when anarchism was active in the country: should there be support for those who resort to "expropriation" or crime in order to support the ideological movement? Or should they be repudiated as discreditable to the libertarian struggle? The intellectuals (mainly those around *La Protesta*) and the anarcho-syndicalists (from the 9th Congress FORA) were strictly opposed to political crime as well as to violence when the latter relied upon recourse to bombs and outrages against individuals. By contrast, the activist groups that advocated "direct action" (the mouthpiece for which was *La Antorcha* from 1921 onwards) and the non-aligned trade union bodies offered moral support to any act, no matter how illegal, directed against "the bourgeois." Furthermore, from 1921 and 1922 onwards, the few anarchists who backed the Russian revolution were well and truly let down by it. The slaughter of black flag supporters by the red-flagged commissars of the new socialist republic—built upon the ruins of the tsarist empire—the deportations and imprisonment of anarchist ideologues who had flooded into Moscow from all corners of the world, had turned the mighty phalanx of working-class anarchism and its thinkers against Lenin and his supporters.

In Argentina, all genuinely anarchist publications lashed the Communist regime and the capitalist regime alike: They were two identical dictatorships, they wrote, different in terms of the ruling classes involved, but they both robbed the people of its freedom. The only contacts between Communists and anarchists in Buenos Aires came through the Italian Anti Fascist Committee made up of exiles of every persuasion to be found in the Italian peninsula. It embraced liberals, socialists, anarchists, and Communists, and together they organized meetings addressed by a speaker from each tendency, which caused grave disagreements to break out between the anarchists. Many of them argued that they could not share a platform with the persecutors of their Russian colleagues.

It was the Italian anarchists most against collaboration with the Communists within the Anti-Fascist Committee who became the two leading figures of expropriator anarchism in Argentina: Miguel Arcángel Roscigna and Severino Di Giovanni.

The Communist mouthpiece *El Internacional* denounced every bomb outrage and every attack and robbery carried out by the anarchists from the "expropriator" faction.

On May 2, 1921, there was an attack on a customs post in Buenos Aires. The raiders got away with a considerable amount of money for those days—620,000 pesetas—but because of a blunder by their driver, Modesto Armeñanzas, the perpetrators were soon found. All but three of them fell into police hands. In the course of their raid, a customs officer had been killed. Of the eleven culprits, three were professional criminals, while the rest were workers who had never broken the law before. Contrary to what certain newspapers may have argued, none of them was an

anarchist, although the raid had reignited the controversy among anarchists themselves regarding approval
or disapproval of any crime committed against the
"bourgeoisie."

Within a few days, Rodolfo González Pacheco
entered the fray when he wrote in an editorial entitled
"Robbers" in *La Antorcha*:

> Since it has been demonstrated that property is
> theft, the only robbers in these parts are the prop-
> erty owners. But what remains to be seen is if those
> who rob them are not of the same ilk as those they
> rob, and do not have a true robbers' mentality, the
> same penchant for acquisition. Let us state that we
> have no prejudice regarding either of them. Espe-
> cially as such a prejudice would protect the former
> even more than they are protected already. Because
> the former shriek: "Stop, thief!" just the way they
> shout "Fatherland and Order!", their sole aim is
> to conceal all their thieving behind all this ver-
> bal brouhaha. Just like the highwayman who fires
> a shot to strike terror, and exploits the chance to
> strip you of your belongings.
>
> No, no, and no. What is happening, in reality?
> What is the robber's object? To seize wealth, or
> at any rate to avoid the toil and the slavery that
> flow from it. In order to escape enslavement, he
> gambles his freedom and generally loses it, in that
> the bourgeoisie are experts in this little game and,
> really, it is they who deal the cards. Should some

petty thief succeed in this game, he becomes rich, a property-owner—which is to say, a big thief.

But for all that, and although they may all be thieves, we are more on the side of the outlaws than of the others, more on the side of the petty thieves than the big ones, more with the customs post raiders than with Yrigoyen and his ministers. May their example prosper!

The expropriator (or illegalist) anarchist group in Argentina arose from the necessity of organizing self-defense. For it was not just the army that cracked down on anarchist activities (Tragic Week, the farm laborers' strike in Patagonia, the dock strike in 1921, etc.) nor just the police (who specialized in combating agitators, arresting ring-leaders, monitoring and breaking up meetings, breaking strikes). There was also, and above all, the nation-wide activity of the Argentine Patriotic League under Carlés's leadership. In those days, not a week passed without some bloody confrontation between anarchist workers and members of the Organization for the Defense of Property, operating under the aegis of the Patriotic League.

The Patriotic League was not merely powerful in the capital, but it was powerful in the interior as well. There, under Carlés's leadership, the landowners and their sons formed themselves into armed phalanxes and underwent military training so they would be prepared to defend themselves against the persistent agitation of the farmworkers. Clashes were inevitable and the one in Gualeguaychú on May 1, 1921 ended in out and out tragedy.

That day, the Patriotic League held a massive demonstration—to counter the workers' planned celebration—with a huge procession of mounted *gauchos*, representatives of the region's Catholic schools, fifty-meter-long Argentinian flags, young girls scattering flowers before the League's burly young men… This demonstration reached its peak with the arrival of Carlés. In frock coat and bowler hat, he climbed out of a biplane that had brought him from Buenos Aires.

Once this High Mass of patriotic display had ended, the gaucho cavalry, under the command of the rancher Francisco Morrogh Bernard, made for the central square in Gualeguaychú where the labor rally was in progress and where both a red and a black flag were flying. At the sight of those emblems, Carlés's men's patriotic blood boiled over. They pounced on the ramshackle proletarian platform and on the three thousand participants. It was carnage. At first, it was believed that five workers and died and thirty-three were seriously wounded. The anarchist press tripled these figures, while the official press minimized them. *La Prensa* tried to explain the episode away by arguing that "95% of the victims were not Argentinians. So one can imagine what sort of labor gathering had taken place, during which anarchists must have violently assailed our nation's symbols. Only 20 to 30 members of the Patriotic League were involved in the incident.

Initially, probably in haste, the police claimed that the workers were not armed."

The following day, two carloads of youths from the Patriotic League attacked the premises of the Drivers' Union in the capital. Two anarchist workers were killed: the Canovi brothers. And three or four days later there was a gunfight at the docks—where the dockers had gone on strike—during which an anarchist worker and a member of the Patriotic League lost their lives.

The violence was escalating, and in their publications the anarchists called for armed resistance to any League attacks and went so far as to advocate "attacking it on its home ground" if necessary.

In the 1920s, it was increasingly difficult to secure a peaceable society. Anarchists bragged about carrying guns—and it's true that they were not shy about using them. One need only cite the Jacinto Aráuz incident where, for the first time in history, a gunfight erupted inside a police station between anarchists and the police. In that case, the farmworkers in the area were living in fear because their rights were being trampled, and anyone who dared protest was replaced by imported labor. The local police inspector could think of no better solution than to invite all parties concerned to the station "for discussions and to come to an agreement." Some workers took up the invitation—among them several delegates influenced by Bakunin's theories—and on their arrival, they were invited to go on through to the station yard, which they were startled to find ringed by armed policemen. There was still no sign of the inspector, and two sergeants began to call the workers one at a time, steering them down a corridor before disarming them and handing them over to other police. They were then made to lie down on the ground and were beaten with clubs. A pretty drastic way of resolving a labor dispute.

But the anarchists who were still in out in the yard and who were assuredly no choirboys themselves opened fire even though they were surrounded. It was a real bloodbath with fatalities on both sides.

From that day forth, Jacinto Aráuz became a symbol for all Argentinian workers. It was, so to speak, an application of the old proverb "what's good for the goose is good for the gander."

Of course, certain anarchists overdid things a bit by always carrying a gun everywhere they went. As it happened, their own publications were moved to openly offer them advice, as in this announcement of a picnic outing to Rosario, carried by *La Antorcha*: "To Rosario, big family picnic to benefit political prisoners, to Castellanos Island on the River Paraná. Gentlemen $1.20, Ladies 50¢, Children free. Note. Let it be known that the sub-prefecturate will be checking passengers before they board, so carrying weapons on one's person is not recommended."

Or indeed this insertion on the front page of *La Protesta*: "Concerning the Sunday picnic: as is, alas, the custom during *La Protesta*-organized picnic outings, shots have been fired into the woods on Maciel Island in the course of the day and particularly as night fell.

This is very dangerous and has panicked some families along on the picnic, which should be a pleasant gathering by anarchists in a spirit of open comradeship. We have had complaints from several participants in the picnic, and even from a fisherman living on the island. All were almost hit by a stray bullet during one of these many shooting sessions. Comrades must avoid firing revolver shots into the woods and impress upon trigger-happy amateurs the danger they are posing. They display utter lack of know-how with these dangerous games, and it is incumbent upon anarchists to oversee the proper progress of our activities and, above all, the safety of all who demonstrate their trust in us by taking part in them. Consequently we urge comrades not to shoot during our picnics and to prevent any participants who may not have read this notice from indulging in the game."

It would appear that this friendly gunfire was a well-established practice, for the newspaper concerned carried the notice for several days in a row.

There were countless instances of clashes between workers of differing persuasions in the workplace; of workers' acts of revolt against foremen or employers, which then degenerated; of wage earners taking on the police and members of the Patriotic League. Let us cite, for example, the case of Pedro Espelocín—who later became an active member of the anarchist expropriator movement—who killed a foreman caught in the act of mistreating a child. There is a long list of political prisoners sentenced for crimes connected with social

and political strife, and these ranged from simply striking to homicide. The Social Prisoners' and Deportees'
Defense Committee, maintained by the modest con-
tributions from anarchist workers, was unable to fully
meet its remit, which was paying the defense counsel fees and the trial expenses of the accused, and also
looking after their families. But this commission did
not have only a passive role that might be summarized
as raising funds, much as some sort of Salvation Army
or society of patronesses might: there was also its secret
brief to help prisoners escape. To that end, it mobilized
all sorts of resources, including sending "trusted comrades" on missions, circling prisons for (sometimes)
months on end so as to gather comprehensive intel-
ligence, renting houses, getting hold of getaway cars,
bribing jailers and court ushers and even the clerks to
do what they could about sentencing.

The man in charge of it all was the secretary of
the Prisoners' and Deportees' Defense Committee
—Miguel Arcángel Roscigna, an anarchist metal-
workers' leader. While the ideologues of *La Protesta*
and *La Antorcha* were pointing out in their columns
that prisoners' freedom ought to be secured only by
means of strikes or by mobilizing the masses of the
people, Roscigna was a man of action sufficiently cun-
ning to thwart the plans of the police and courts. He
was a cerebral, cool, scheming sort. But when action
was called for, he was the one who took the bull by
the horns, not just by leading, but also by springing
into action. He had demonstrated this already in the

Radowitzky case: he had patiently and adroitly made overtures so that he might be appointed a prison guard in Ushuaia. There he was to prepare everything in fine detail so that this time the escape attempt would not fail. Just as everything was in place, a blabbermouth at the congress of the Argentine Union of Trade Unions, made up of socialist and trade unionist leaders, hell-bent upon doing the anarchists damage, disclosed that Roscigna was 'working as a "dog" in Ushuaia prison' ("dog" being the affectionate nickname that anarchists used for prison guards and policemen). Inquiries were made, and the police discovered that Roscigna was indeed on Tierra del Fuego. He was immediately sacked and driven from the prison. Before he vanished and lest all his trouble should have been for nothing, Roscigna torched the prison governor's home.

Later it was Roscigna who orchestrated the initial escape of the baker Ramón Silveyra who had been sentenced to twenty years in prison. And laid the groundwork for Silveyra's second breakout. Those two genuinely sensational events demonstrated his real flair as organizer—a flair that he later demonstrated in the preparation of sensational attacks and in direct action operations.

The relentless war being waged between the two anarchists factions, the *protestistas* and the *antochistas*, the right- and left-wings of the movement, became so frenzied that the Defense Committee split into two factions, each championing its own prisoners. The factions close to *La Protesta* and the 5th Congress FORA would support only anarchist prisoners of conscience, whereas the one close to *La Antorcha* was to leap to the defense of all prisoners accused of criminal offenses (which is to say, the anarchist expropriators). And that is what happened in the highly controversial case of the Viedma prisoners.

In 1923, in the Río Negro region, a mail coach was attacked, just like in the Wild West. The territorial police arrested five anarchist farm laborers not too far from the scene as they were collecting firewood for an *asado*.[10] Under atrocious torture, they confessed to the attack. One of them, Casiano Ruggerone, was driven mad as a result of the torture and died a few months later in the asylum in Vieytes. The other four were sentenced to a total of eighty-three years in prison. Andrés Gómez got twenty-five years, as did Manuel Viegas and Manuel Álvarez, whilst Esteban Hernando got eight years.

The faction close to *La Antorcha* waged a protracted campaign to have the case reviewed. *La Protesta*, having shown itself lukewarm in their defense wrote in its columns that the Viedma prisoners "are ordinary offenders who have nothing to do with anarchist propaganda and anarchist ideas." This inflamed the polemic within the movement, a polemic that was to linger for as long as anarchism played a role of any significance in Argentine labor life. Moreover, it has been a constantly recurring theme in anarchism:

---

10   *Asado* is the beef barbecue of which Argentinians are so fond.

since Proudhon and passing through Bakunin, Reclus, Malatesta, Armand, Gori, Fabbri, Treni, Abad de Santillán. How many have queried whether all means are legitimate in the making of the revolution, or whether anarchists should cling to the image of pure and irreproachable figures who make the revolution by preaching a humanistic ideal?!

Little by little, events brought the two schools of thought into grave paradoxes, in, say, the Sacco-Vanzetti affair—a case of injustice that, in terms of the worldwide labor mobilization it provoked, had a greater impact than the Dreyfus Affair in its day.[11]

What happened to Sacco and Vanzetti? Almost the same thing that happened to the Viedma prisoners, except that in the latter case, what we today would describe as "public opinion" was not a factor. By contrast, Vanzetti and his Italian anarchist comrades in the United States managed to make masterly use of popular opinion over more than seven years of a worldwide popular agitation, which will probably never be equaled. In the United States itself, the agitation was on a scale ten times that of the agitation that would subsequently lead to the end of the Vietnam War.

---

11   Alfred Dreyfus was a Jewish officer in the French army, unjustly accused, in the 1890s, of spying for Germany. In the face of all the evidence, the French army, the Right, and the Catholic community refused to absolve Dreyfus and convict the true culprit, one of their own, as the "honor" of the Army was by then at stake. Known simply as "The Affair," the scandal radically divided French and world public opinion. Dreyfus was eventually and grudgingly cleared.

In the Sacco-Vanzetti case, there was unanimity between everyone, individualist anarchists,
anarcho-communists, anarchist expropriators and
devotees of violence, social democrats, Communists,
liberals, the Pope, and even the fascists who "endorsed
the judge's decision to suspend the death sentences
on the accused."[12]

Once arrested—fifteen days after the Braintree
hold-up and the killing of two cashiers—Sacco and
Vanzetti said that they had been indirectly implicated
in the raid. Their confessions had been made on the
advice of their lawyer who believed that this would
save them from deportation to Italy, which would also
be their immediate fate should they confess to being
anarchists. To put it another way, in their case there
was none of the physical torture used on the Viedma
prisoners, but rather pressure and mental torment:
either they accepted the legal niceties or they would
be extradited. And despite support from all over the
world this was an interminable bluff that they were
fated to lose after seven long years.

The courts disgraced themselves by sentencing
Sacco and Vanzetti to the electric chair. At no point
were the US judges able to demonstrate with clar-
ity that the two Italians were guilty. There were only

---

12   Benito Mussolini's appeal was made solely in order to win the
     sympathy of the Italian community in the United States; while
     at home, he himself was harassing anarchists, communists, and
     socialists with frequent recourse to castor oil, imprisonment, ex-
     ile, and, as in the Matteotti affair, political murder.

legally worthless and inconclusive suggestions and testimony. It goes without saying that what tipped the scales, above all else, in the sentencing was the fact that the accused were anarchists. It was the same in the Viedma prisoners' case. As for Sacco and Vanzetti's guilt or innocence, we will never be able to pronounce on that with certainty. On the other hand, there is no denying that they were members of a pro-direct-action group. *L'Adunata dei Refrattari* was the mouthpiece of the New York Italian anarchists, to whom we are largely indebted for the launching of the mammoth worldwide campaign that sounded the alarm. This was a newspaper unambiguous in its support for direct action. So much so that a few years later it would support Severino Di Giovanni and his colleagues who were to be either ignored or damned in Argentina. The last word on the Sacco-Vanzetti case might well be that delivered by the journalist and writer Francis Russell in his painstaking investigation entitled *Tragedy in Dedham* (published in 1962 and hailed as a serious study by the entire European press). Francis Russell reckons—and James Joll shares this view—that Sacco was a dyed-in-the-wool "expropriator" and went in for that sort of thing as a means of raising funds for the cause. And the likelihood is that he and Vanzetti—who was always welcoming towards the persecuted, without asking whether they were expropriators or not—were framed because they were dangerous agitators.

But there was nevertheless a hiccup in the support that anarchists gave Sacco and Vanzetti. Should they be defended as innocents or because they were anarchists? And, if they actually were guilty of hold-ups designed to finance propaganda or to help prisoners and strikers, would they have had the same championship from the columns of the "official journals" of Argentinian anarchists? The same dilemma recurred with Buenaventura Durruti's exploits in Argentina.

On October 18, 1925, three persons slipped "movie-style," as *La Prensa* put it, into the Las Heras tram depot in Anglo, smack dab in the middle of the Palermo district. One of them wore a mask. The cashiers had just finished counting the money from ticket sales. "Hands up!" the shout rang out in a strong Spanish accent before the money was demanded. The stammering employees explained that the cash was already in the safe. The key was demanded, to no avail, as the manager had left and taken it with him. The raiders conferred with one another and withdrew. As they slipped past the cash-desk, they grabbed a small bag that a guard had just set down. It held 38 pesos, in ten-centavo coins. Waiting outside, was an accomplice and, a little further off, a car was waiting. They vanished without a trace.

The man who had just spearheaded this fruitless raid, which netted only 38 pesos in small change (which was obviously a disappointing result for the raiders who had acted with mathematical precision, but overlooked one tiny detail), was none other than Buenaventura Durruti. The same Durruti who, eleven years later, became the most legendary personality of the Spanish Civil War, the unchallenged leader of the Spanish anarchists and libertarians from around the world who came to defend the Republic against the Francoist rebels. Durruti, commander of a column of the same name, who came from Aragon to rescue Madrid, and who, with his three-thousand poorly trained militians, defeated an entire disciplined army complete with staff officers and uniformed generals who had made a study of tactics, strategy, and command.

This gunman with his 380 ten-centavo coins was the man who, after he perished in the "University City" in Madrid, had the most grandiose funeral ever bestowed upon any workers' leader in Spain. James Joll said:

> Durruti's death robbed the anarchists of one of their most celebrated and ruthless heroes. His funeral, held in Barcelona, was the last great anarchist show of strength, drawing two hundred thousand militants who paraded through the streets of the city. One would have thought one was at the demonstration played out in Moscow fourteen years earlier when the funeral of Kropotkin offered the Russian anarchists their last chance of a public show of strength, before the Communists wiped them out.

And, by an irony of fate, or because ideologues have to adapt to circumstance, the anarchist intellectual

Diego Abad de Santillán—one of the Argentinian libertarian militants most outspoken in his criticism of the "expropriators"—referred, in 1969, to the 38-peso bandit thus: "Buenaventura Durruti, the fearless knight beyond reproach."

The Buenos Aires police were bewildered: bandits with Spanish accents? They had no such people on their books. They interrogated people from the milieu and came up empty handed. Nobody knew them. As they had netted a derisory sum, the police suspected that they would soon give it another try.

And indeed they did on November 17, 1925—barely a month after the raid on the Las Heras depot.

A few minutes before midnight, Durand, the counter clerk at the Primera Junta metro station in Caballito, was finishing checking the day's receipts. He was just waiting for the takings from the last metro and his shift would be over. Suddenly a stranger stepped up, slowly drawing a handgun, and told him in a Spanish accent: "Shut it!", while another one burst into the kiosk and grabbed a wooden cash box where the takings were usually kept. It was all over in a flash. The strangers turned on their heels and made for the Centenera Street exit. Counter clerk Durand began to shout at the top of his voice: "Help! Thief!" One of the raiders turned and fired into the air to scare him. A policeman standing at the junction of Rivadavia and Centenera streets heard the shouting and gunfire and came running with his weapon drawn. But two accomplices were keeping watch on the two approaches to the metro station, and seeing the policeman, one of them drew his gun, fired twice and hit the mark.

The policeman dropped to the ground. The four raiders raced to the taxi that was waiting for them at the corner of Rosario and Centenera streets, but the driver could not get the engine to start and after a few agonizing minutes' delay, the strangers got out of the car, ran east down Rosario Street, and vanished.

The raid was a waste of time: like the Las Heras raid it was a shambles. The takings had not been left, as was the custom, in the wooden cash box, but rather were in a steel box under the counter. The wooden box did not contain as much as a single ten-centavo piece.

The situation was getting serious. As far as the police could see, the Caballito raiders were the same as in the Las Heras depot raid: same modus operandi, same accents. This time though, a police officer had been killed, a Sergeant Núñez.

The Chilean police had just sent the Argentinian police photographs and the court dossier on a gang of robbers of Spanish, Mexican, and Cuban extraction, which had stolen 46,923 Chilean pesos from the Mataderos branch of the Bank of Chile on July 16 that year. After grabbing the money, persons unknown had sped from the scene in a car, firing shots in the air and causing considerable mayhem in the busy district. One bank clerk had managed to grab on to the car just as it pulled away. One of the raiders screamed at him to get down, and shot him dead when he failed to comply.

Armed with these details, the Chilean police informed their Argentinian counterparts that the gang comprised five men, one of whom had sailed from Valparaiso for France, while the other four had made for Argentina. The boarding house where they had been living in Santiago de Chile was found. The landlady said that "the five men were polite and spoke continually about social struggles. They professed to be Spanish revolutionaries and were touring the countries of America in search of funds destined to overthrow the monarchy in Spain."

Those who had crossed into Argentina had papers in the names of Ramón Carcano Caballero (Mexican), José Manuel Labrada Pontón (Cuban), Manuel Serrano García (a Spaniard from Valencia), and Teodoro Pichardo Ramos (another Mexican).

The Argentinian police compared the photographs with the eye-witness statements about the Las Heras depot and Primera Juna raiders. There could be no doubt; they were one and the same. At that point, an interminable investigation was launched; boarding houses, hotels, and guest houses were searched. Nothing. The Social Order Department also went into operation, arresting anarchist activists in search of a few clues, but came up empty handed.

The photos of the four foreigners were plastered over every metro carriage and in the trams.[13] In the wake of the Primera Junta raid, *La Prensa* gave the

---

13   The fifth was being sought in Chile and France.

following description of the raiders: "Everyone who saw the malefactors yesterday is agreed that they were persons of respectable appearance. They were dressed formally and there was nothing in their appearance to arouse suspicion. If anything, they had an attractive look about them."

The police came up with two hypotheses: either they had moved on to Uruguay or Brazil right after the raid, or, having failed to make anything out of the two armed robberies, they had gone into hiding before launching a further operation. It transpired that the second hypothesis was the right one.

"Just as the residents of the peaceable town of San Martín were getting ready to go out to lunch, or had retreated into their homes to escape the rigors of the sunshine and the heat, a gang of armed outlaws posted themselves by the entrance to the Provincial bank branch facing the main square." That was how *La Prensa*, on January 19, 1926, opened its account of the famous stick-up of the San Martín bank, which inspired so much comment at the time.

Seven persons unknown (four of them masked) got out of a Phaeton automobile on the corner of Buenos Aires and Belgrano streets, two hundred meters from the police station. Four of them went into the bank while the other three, wielding carbines, took up positions by the main door. This was a raid of a singular sort, in best gangster style. A pedestrian who happened by immediately had their guns trained on him. At the beginning, passers-by thought that it was a hoax, but they quickly learned otherwise, at which point they scampered away like rabbits. Inside, the four strangers were busy; they walked behind the counters, emptying the tills and collecting all the money they found. They gathered up 64,085 pesos, and that was without even taking the trouble to tackle the safe. The bank staff cooperated from the moment the raiders entered when they heard a raucous voice with a Spanish accent call out to them: "Move and we drop you!"

Two staff members, who were hiding behind the counter, tried to crawl out the back door on all fours. The masked men spotted them, and unhesitatingly fired, killing the employee Rafael Ruiz and wounding his colleague.

Their job complete, they fled by car with the proceeds. Pursued, they covered their withdrawal by firing shots and did not skimp on the gunpowder.

The police were now confronted by something different; this time the numbers of the raiders left them puzzled: seven, plus a driver. If this was the gang from Chile, it had found itself fresh help. It was right in the middle of the investigation that the Central Police Department got its big break. With tension running very high, journalists were called to a press conference. The Barcelona police authorities suggested likely candidates for the four who had raided the Las Heras tram depot, the Primera Junta, and the Bank of Chile. They were neither Mexicans nor Cubans, the Barcelona police recounted, but Spaniards and the four names they had given were false. Their real identities were as follows:

Ramon Carcano Caballero was in fact one Buenaventura Durruti, born in the city of León on July 14, 1886, a driver by profession.

Teodoro Pichardo Ramos was Francisco Ascaso, a native of Almudévar in the province of Huesca, born on April 2, 1902.

Manuel Labrada Pontón was in fact Alejandro Ascaso, a native of Almudévar—like his above-named brother—born on October 17, 1889. Manuel Serrano García's real name was Gregorio Jover Cortés, and he was born in Valencia in 1892.

The Barcelona police added that this was "a dangerous gang of anarchists long active in Barcelona where it has carried out a large number of armed attacks, robberies, and murders." What is more, Francisco Ascaso was believed to have killed Cardinal Soldevila in Zaragoza.

Later, with the aid of Mexican and Cuban police, the trajectory of the Spanish anarchist gang was reconstructed: it opened with the attack on the Bank of Gijón in Spain, a raid designed to raise money to fund the struggle against the Primo de Rivera dictatorship. From Gijón they went to Mexico and passed through Carolina, where they pulled off a hold-up, even though one of their number was killed. From there they moved on to Cuba where they successfully raided another bank.

They left Havana aboard the steamer *Oriana*, which took them as far as Valparaiso in Chile, where they arrived on June 9, 1925. There they plied a number of trades until, on July 11, they attacked the Bank of Chile in Santiago. They returned to laboring until the beginning of August when they caught the train for Buenos Aires.

Everything was clear. All that was left was to catch them. It became a matter of international prestige. The certainty that they were dealing with anarchists focused investigations upon the ideological faction known for its advocacy of violence and expropriation. Moreover, all routes by which Durruti might leave the country were under close surveillance.

But it was the French police and not the Argentinian who would have the satisfaction of arresting him.

Five months after the San Martín bank raid, a cable from Paris reported that French police had thwarted an anarchist attempt on the life of Alfonso XIII, king of Spain, during his visit to France. Two Spanish anarchists, Francisco Ascaso and another who went by the name of Durruti had been arrested in a modest hotel in Clichy with plans and weapons proving their intention to mount a serious attempt upon the life of the Spanish monarch.

This news set the Argentinian police buzzing: they hoped to have revenge for Sergeant Núñez, shot down during the Primera Junta raid. They made overtures to their French colleagues to discover in greater detail precisely how Francisco Ascaso and Durruti had arrived in France, on what passports. They also asked them to try to arrest Jover Cortés and Ascaso's brother as well.

The Paris police replied that Francisco Ascaso had landed from a ship in Cherbourg on April 30, 1926, as had Durruti. A few days later, the French police succeeded in arresting Jover too. All three men carried Uruguayan passports: the first was in the name of José Cotelo, the second in that of Salvador Arévalo, and the third in the name of Luis Victorio Repetto. The three passports had been issued by the Uruguayan embassy in Buenos Aires. For the Argentinian police, that sealed it. José Cotelo was a Uruguayan anarchist and resident of Buenos Aires. They picked him up a short time after that. Cotelo acknowledged that, on April 1, he had taken out a Uruguayan passport in his own name, but claimed to have lost it within hours, it having probably fallen out of his pocket. Such simplistic tales could hardly do anything other than exasperate detectives who threatened to make him pay the price for the depredation done by Durruti and company. But Cotelo kept quiet. The other two surnames, Arévalo and Repetto, were likewise the names of two Uruguayan anarchist activists operating in Buenos Aires. The former worked at a bakery, but neither he nor Repetto could be found. The court released Cotelo after hundreds of fruitless interrogation sessions and several weeks in the cells.

However, the Argentine police had not given up, and were counting on securing Durruti's, Ascaso's, and Jover's extraditions. High-ranking police officers sought out President Alvear himself to ask him to use his influence with Paris—where he had been the ambassador for many years—to have the anarchists handed over quickly. To speed things up, three of Buenos Aires's finest sleuths—Fernández Bazán, Romero, and Carrasco—were dispatched to Paris. The embassy formally applied to the French government for extradition. After a lot of red tape and delay, the French caved in and told the Argentinian ambassador in Paris, Álvarez de Toledo, that Durruti, Ascaso, and Jover would be at their disposal. An Argentinian navy warship, the *Bahía Blanca*, then set sail to bring them back to Buenos Aires.

The anarchists—through *La Antorcha*—denounced this as a conspiracy by the Argentine, French, and Spanish governments. They wrote: "In the sordid conspiracy in which the fate of three men—our comrades Ascaso, Durruti, and Jover—is at stake like in any game with loaded dice, there is, in addition to the visible players, another player who pretends not to be playing but who really supervises the others. That player is Spain. To save face, France has refused to extradite to Spain, because they have no extradition treaty. But governments always stick by one another when it comes to hunting down subversives, and so France is acceding indirectly to her request by granting extradition to Argentina. In this way, France kills two birds with one stone: in return for the extradition, her government obtains from Argentina a re-scheduling of the war debt incurred in the purchase of wheat, and at the same time, curries favor with the Spanish government, which is hopeful of obtaining from Argentina—should she decide not to proceed with charges—the extradition of the three

Spaniards, because an extradition treaty does exist between these two countries." The newspaper closed with these words: *Tutti contenti* (Everybody's happy).

When the three young anarchists discovered that they were to be handed over to the Argentine police, they took the news calmly, knowing that they had to get to work right now without wasting a minute, and they did to everything they could think of: hunger strikes, protest campaigns, calls for solidarity, and petitions from the anarchist movements around the world. A formidable campaign was launched on behalf of Ascaso, Durruti, and Jover, and for a time it met with such success that it overshadowed the concurrent one mounted on behalf of Sacco and Vanzetti.

"Ascaso, Durruti, and Jover, the new Sacco and Vanzetti," wrote the anarchist newspapers around the globe. In Argentina, the impact was immediate: rallies were organized, and a pamphlet was published[14] that asserted the three had never been to Argentina, that the alleged hold-ups were no more than concoctions and inventions designed to cover up the Argentine police's failures.

In France, all of the press, except for the right-wing press, called for the release of the three anarchists, and denounced the iniquity of extradition. French intellectuals (liberals, socialists, communists, and anarchists of every hue) signed petitions on behalf of "there brave

---

14   The initial print run of twenty thousand copies of this pamphlet sold out within a week, and another run of thirty thousand was immediately printed.

men who seek only that their homeland be free." In France, in the National Assembly, the campaign was taken up and socialist deputies tabled a bill to overhaul the law on extradition.

The French government wavered. It had too many problems at home to go looking for more, so it contrived an *impasse* and shifted its position by making extradition orders conditional upon fulfillment of certain legal procedures. The first round had been won, but the Argentinian police put pressure on President Alvear, and they were determined not to lose this time. In Buenos Aires, the police banned any demonstration in favor of the three anarchists. *La Antorcha*, the Social Prisoners' Defense Committee, and the non-aligned[15] trade unions of the bakers, plasterers, painters, drivers, carpenters, footwear industry workers, car valets, and bronze polishers, the Italian groups' Liaison Committee (led by Severino Di Giovanni and Aldo Aguzzi), and the Bulgarian group defied the police threats and held impromptu rallies. In this regard, the anarchists were, so to speak, a race apart. Their methods were truly singular: for instance, they scheduled and announced a demonstration in the Once Square. Naturally, the police flooded the area and scattered the small body of demonstrators. At that point, an anarchist stepped out

---

15   Nonaligned-trade-unions (*gremios autónomos*). The term *gremio* was used in those days to mean a craft union as well as its premises, or a trade union (*sociedad de resistencia*) in the FORA (Federación Obrera Regional Argentina). Here, nonaligned-trade-unions seems the best translation.

of the metro station beside the Once Square and two others quickly chained him to the railings. The police could no longer bundle the anarchist away. He began to harangue the crowd in a booming voice, the sort one would have heard at a gathering where there was no public address system: "Over here! The anarchists are here to shout out the truth about comrades Durruti, Jover, and Ascaso."

The police raced over to find the dizzying spectacle of a man crucified with chains, his words spitting out like machine-gun fire. While they conferred and orders flew to and fro, the anarchist carried on shouting at the dumbfounded, open-mouthed onlookers.

The police's first reaction was to beat him into silence, but as the anarchist carried on with his harangue, that became a most inappropriate spectacle. The beating of a man who was bound and defenseless was offensive to more than one onlooker. Their second reaction was to gag him, which proved quite an undertaking, for the anarchist put up a fight and snatches of sentences still escaped his lips, creating an even more grotesque spectacle that attracted more spectators. In the end, the police had to resign themselves to waiting patiently for the arrival of a Black Maria from the Central Department, which took a full hour to saw through his chains. Meanwhile, of course, our orator had delivered three or four speeches, covering everything form Ascaso, Durruti, and Jover to Sacco and Vanzetti, not forgetting Radowitzky and the Viedma prisoners. He berated Alvear (whom anarchists referred to as "the street-walker" or the "hundred kilos of butter"), the police ("these braying asses, these brutes"), Carlés ("the honorable bastard"), the members of the Patriotic League ("these daddy's boys, these homosexual scum"), Leopoldo Lugones ("this crook-beaked bird of somber plumage"), Communism ("this authoritarian cretinism"), the military ("these stupid gorillas"), etc. sparing no one, as we can see!

Defense of Durruti and his comrades was—like it or not—defense of expropriator anarchism, of the right that libertarians awarded themselves to "expropriate" in order to make revolution. Anarchists of the *antorchista* school were very well aware that Durruti had come to Argentina to carry out three armed robberies, which is why the moral defense they employed in this instance was somewhat ambivalent: They had always maintained that the trio was innocent and incapable of committing criminal acts. To put that another way, they did not defend them as revolutionaries and did not attempt to justify what they had done, but merely repeated: they are innocent, further victims of bourgeois justice.

Interesting to note that *La Antorcha*, while favorably disposed to violent action, defended those who practiced it by representing them as gentle lambs. It persisted with this language through all these years of violence, up until it ceased publication in 1932. In Argentina, there was only one publication that sided openly with expropriation and action rooted in violence: that was the Italian-language newspaper

Culmine, published by Severino Di Giovanni.[16]

We might note too that whereas in France the whole liberal intelligentsia and liberal-minded political organizations mobilized in defense of Durruti, Ascaso, and Jover, Argentinian anarchism was a house divided against itself. The moderates of *La Protesta*, led by López Arango and Abad de Santillán, wrote in an editorial towards the end of 1926: "The protests against the extradition of Ascaso, Durruti and Jover do not qualify for the description anarchist." Those comments signaled the beginning of a war to the death declared by the doyen of the Argentine anarchist press against those who, within the movement, championed armed assault, robbery, or counterfeiting as ways of making revolution.

In April 1927, the French government overruled the popular threats and protests and resolved to confirm the three Spaniards' extradition. The Paris appeal court did likewise. The Argentinian police were jubilant.

The game was up. *La Antorcha* bemoaned the news by declaring: "Go to hell, ye gentlemen politicians of this prostituted France which traffics in human lives!"

It railed against France as well as Argentina, which it described as a "barbarous country with neither laws nor individual and collective guarantees, wide open to every abuse and any sort of violence. Such is Argentina." And later: "Argentina is an immeasurably stupid

---

16   See the note on Severino Di Giovanni after this essay.

country, bereft of moral conscience and the slightest sense of injustice. In this country, only a sordid fear rules and an even more sordid one obeys. The only values are cowardice, falsehood, and villainy."

The Argentinian ambassador in Paris, Álvarez de Toledo, informed the French government that he would take charge of the prisoners as quickly as possible and that an Argentinian warship would dock in Le Havre to take them on board. Needless to say, the French and Argentinian anarchist press vented their anger on Álvarez de Toledo. *La Antorcha* ran exposés of the "trickery practiced against the public administration" and accused Alvear of having bought the extraditions by rescheduling the war debts France had incurred through the purchase of foodstuffs.

The Social Prisoners' Defense Committee prepared to defend the three Spaniards once they landed on Argentinian soil. The Committee alerted the public that International Red Aid would also be leaping to the defense of Durruti and his comrades, but that no one had asked it to do any such thing, since the prisoners were anarchists and had nothing to do with the Communists. Moreover, the Committee pointed out to International Red Aid members that they would be better employed defending anarchists imprisoned in Russia.

The agitation created by the Ascaso, Durruti, and Jover case increased in intensity in Buenos Aires, and was added to the Sacco and Vanzetti campaign. Alvear realized that, once they had landed, the three Spaniards would be yet another burr under the saddle of a labor movement that was already greatly overwrought in that year, 1927. Did they have to come? Why? Merely to satisfy the police? Alvear was shrewder than the Americans who had had their fingers burned by the Sacco-Vanzetti affair and provoked the wrath of the entire world. Was it really worth the trouble to drag three Spaniards back to stand trial in Argentina? No, definitely not. He already had enough problems with Radowitzky in Ushuaia, and was disinclined to go looking for more and give the anarchists a fresh excuse for planting bombs, organizing more demonstrations, and unleashing further strikes. Alvear knew that the anarchists were lying when they said that Durruti and his colleagues were three little angels and had done nothing in Argentina. He also took the line that the police were right to want vengeance for a colleague's death. But the fact was that the arrests made in France had been made not in connection with an ordinary criminal offence, but with a political offence, in that it had involved plans to take the life of the weakling Alfonso XIII.

And it was all signed and sealed in a highly diplomatic fashion: France gave Argentina a three-month period during which to make provisions for the passage of the accused. Argentina delayed her answer and asked that the prisoners be delivered aboard a French Navy escort ship, arguing that she would not have a vessel available at the time. The French government refused the request and the days dragged by. At that point, the Argentinian government conveyed its displeasure with the French government: if the prisoners were not delivered, it would be France's fault. And vice versa: if the prisoners failed to leave France, it would be down to the negligence of the Argentinian government. The days passed and the period of grace expired. Deep down, everyone was happy to be rid of the problem. Ascaso, Durruti, and Jover were freed in Paris, and then promptly deported to Belgium.

For the anarchists, of course, this was a victory that provided an occasion for great celebrations. So they were measured in their remarks and gratification. *La Antorcha* wrote an article entitled "Deliverance," which read,

> The battle between the French and Argentinian peoples and their respective governments and police forces has ended with the latter's being obliged to quit the field, in deference to the cause of freedom and justice. The governments are disguising their defeat by invoking the usual pretexts required to salvage *raison d'état*. The French government, on the pretext that it is awaiting passage of a law on the matter, has yielded to pubic opinion by repeatedly dropping the extradition proceedings. And the Argentinian government, fearing the vigorous popular pressure at home and abroad that would have resulted, has not pressed the point. And so Ascaso, Durruti, and Jover have been released and the two governments and police forces pretend that they have not suffered any defeat. As in chess, the game is abandoned when checkmate is

inevitable. We have rescued three of our comrades over whom awful menaces were hanging. We are overwhelmed by a surge of delight at the sight of our action succeeding and the reactionaries routed. This is a double delight from which we can draw fresh courage to press on with the struggle today, and tomorrow to press ahead with the struggle to release all our people, Sacco and Vanzetti, Radowitzky, etc. Meanwhile, the police, tormented by their defeat and furious about it, are preparing to make us pay dearly for our victory and their defeat the moment we display any weakness. Let us strive to ensure that the sharp teeth of these rabid dogs bite the dust, by inflicting further defeats upon them, which will be victories for us, the people.

Durruti and his comrades would carry on with their struggle too, but would not return to Argentina (although in 1933 the police, by design or accident, mentioned them in connection with a stick-up at the Bank of London in Flores). But although they never returned, their influence upon expropriator anarchism was crucial.

In the San Martín hold-up, Durruti had been flanked by two Argentinian anarchists: Miguel Arcángel Roscigna and Andrés Vázquez Paredes. Both were to be protagonists of the most celebrated raid of the 1920s—the Rawson Hospital raid.

How did it come to pass that Miguel Arcángel Roscigna, a highly qualified metalworker—a wrought iron specialist—prized by his employer on account of his appetite for hard work and good application, in spite of his trade union and political militancy, should have turned to armed robbery? He enjoyed a happy family life—he was a good father and had a home that was modest but had every comfort.

Who was this Roscigna? What sort of a person was he? One of his comrades, Gino Gatti, wrote: "Viewed with the benefit of hindsight, the life of Miguel Arcángel Roscigna was a veritable epic poem, a paean to solidarity." Emilio Uriondo, one of the staunchest anarchists, who grew up alongside Roscigna, said that he was "the most intelligent of all the activist anarchists, the most selfless, a man who, in bourgeois life, could have had a comfortable and peaceable life for himself, but who opted instead to let it all go and stake his life for his ideals." Even Abad de Santillán, the enemy of the expropriators, said that Roscigna was "an intelligent, determined, and unselfish fellow. Which is why we were sorry to see him caught up in matters that could not but lead him to perdition."

Just like Severino Di Giovanni, an anarchist who gave his ideals priority over all else, who regarded as enemies all who were not themselves anarchists (and even those who were but who did not go in for direct action as he interpreted it), Roscigna was a cerebral type who threw himself into social struggles as the best way to combat the established order. But upon two points Roscigna would make no compromise: his attitude towards the police (according to former members of the Social Order branch, Roscigna, Nicola Recchi, and Umberto Lanciotti could stand up to any torture) and his dealings with the Communists.

In May 1925, Roscigna published an essay called "Maverick Anarchists" in which he was scathing about Italian anarchists who were members of the Anti-Fascist Committee alongside socialists, liberals, and Communists: "At present, it defies belief that there should be one anarchist left capable of action and ignorant of what the Communist Party is and aspires to be. Thousands of comrades dead, imprisoned, and outlawed—such is the sinister record of the government which in Russia wields a dictatorship every bit as iniquitous as that of the fascists in Italy."

And he went further, saying: "Are the comrades not aware of the tradition of opprobrium and the noxious handiwork of these damned shepherds within the rebel workers' organizations in our country? Will they at least acknowledge the Communists' handiwork in dampening social strife during the unforgettable episode of the factory occupations? Do they not know about the daily butchery which fastens, like some re-enacted Kronstadt, silently and inexorably upon any hint of potential opposition, or mere challenge to orders emanating from Russia's new masters, even should that opposition be articulated by those creators of communism who may wish to remain true to their ideals?"

He concluded with a statement of opposition to all alliance with those who "in contrast with our

designs upon freedom, peddle nothing but authority."
This staunchly anti-communist line of anarchism's
fighting leftwing would be taken further later—among
one faction and with encouragement from Horacio
Badaraco (a member of the *La Antorcha* communion,
unjustly forgotten today).

In July 1927, anarchists caused panic among all
who had any US connections, all because of the Sacco
and Vanzetti affair. There was a flurry of terrorist
attacks. The police view was that the instigator of this
activity was the Italian, Severino Di Giovanni, but
they had nagging suspicions about the apparently lev-
elheaded anarchist Miguel Arcángel Roscigna. On July
24, he made the mistake of spending the night in his
own home at 4585 César Díaz Street, which is where
detectives from the Social Order branch arrested him.
They were very well aware that they had no evidence
against him, but they wanted to "test the water." Furthermore, they had had reports from the Uruguayan
police to the effect that Roscigna and Emilio Uriondo
had been behind a bomb attack on the United States
embassy in Uruguay, and prepared a book bomb—a
real masterpiece apparently—for sending to the governor of Ushuaia penitentiary.

They held Roscigna at the Social Order bureau
for several days, but all they got out of him were
lies: innocently, he told them that he had renounced
his anarchist beliefs, that his participation in labor
struggles was in his younger days, and that, now thir-
ty-six years old, he was devoting his time to studying

poultry-farming preparatory to setting up a farm.

With men like him who never admitted anything, the police had two courses of action open to them: either to liquidate them on the spot (under the Bazán law) or to release them and tail them in the hope of catching them red-handed, so that no judge could free them on the basis of insufficient evidence. The Social Order officers involved in the hunt for Severino Di Giovanni gave up on Roscigna. That was a serious error on their part, one that soon brought them plenty of headaches and made them the laughing-stock of the population barely two months later.

When the courts released him, on the grounds of insufficient evidence, Roscigna felt like he had been given a new lease on life, but he knew that his days were numbered. Inspector Buzzo's adjutant had plainly told him: "You have three options: take yourself off to La Quiaca and raise chickens, enter a seminary and study for the priesthood, or commit suicide without delay, which would make life easier for us, because the next time we come across you in some street in Buenos Aires, we'll bump you off and place a gun in your hand and say you were resisting the authorities!"

But Roscigna had other fish to fry: help for anarchist prisoners was in a disastrous state, because the money had run out. Thus, for lack of funds, the daily dispatch of food parcels to Caseros[17] and La Peniten-

---

17   Caseros, a Buenos Aires prison on Caseros Avenue.

ciaria—parcels that cost no less than 100 pesos per month per head—had been suspended. Aid payments had been cut to 8 or 10 pesos weekly. This help was distributed to all anarchist inmates without distinction, whether they had been convicted or were merely in custody at the Central Department. In spite of these cuts, it was still a terrible drain on resources, for aid had still to be found for the families of prisoners and fugitives. Moreover, Roscigna was not prepared to make do with passively helping those awaiting trial. His concern was to free comrades, even if they were being held in some impregnable place. But to do that, as we have said, it took a lot of money. And while Roscigna was a dyed-in-the-wool optimist, he was also a pragmatist: "Drastic problem? Drastic remedy!"

In the execution of his plans, he had learned a lot from the few months he had spent with Durruti. Solidarity collections simply had to continue and the workers had to give their last penny for the comrades behind bars. Such collections stimulated fraternal feelings and created a revolutionary moral obligation. But action was also needed and money had to be raised through expropriation operations, without any sort of scruples about those who spent their lives profiteering while others suffered.

Roscigna wanted to plan things down to the finest detail so that the operation would be worthwhile and bring in a good sum without needless trouble. He was relying on his devoted friend, the self-assured, intelligent, and far-sighted young Spaniard, Andrés Vázquez

Paredes. The latter had, to his credit, a very active record of struggle in the painters' union, was expert in bomb-making, and had been in prison following involvement in the terrorist attacks of 1921 at the time of the campaign in support of Radowitzky. This was the same Vázquez Paredes who had helped the German anarchist Kurt Wilckens prepare the bomb that killed Lieutenant Colonel Varela. But while Roscigna could depend on Vázquez Paredes, there was another vital assistant missing: Emilio Uriondo, who was being held in the Punta Carretas prison in Montevideo in connection with the US embassy bombing.

Emilio Uriondo proves wrong those who argue that the entire anarchist movement in Argentina was made up of foreigners. He in fact was a purebred *criollo*, Emilio Adelmo Uriondo, from the Magdalena district. His person boasted all that is prized in the native born: the nobility of one who never deserts his friends or the principles of loyalty when they are in jeopardy, a man of integrity, always staunch. Possessed of those qualities, he also had the *criollos'* sixth sense for guessing who was who. He deployed this acuity of mind in his dealings with the police and with the authorities, because, good *criollo* that he was, he was a rebel, a die-hard. He did not like to be bossed about or manhandled. By what right would he be bossed around? The *criollo* belief was that the only blessing God had bestowed upon man was his freedom, a sacred word. Emilio Uriondo needed that freedom because he respected other men's freedom. He was possessed of the typical *criollo* culture. He was refined, even delicate of speech. And was, in addition, capable of bearing any physical pain. His broad shoulders would bear the brunt of several years in Ushuaia, and the beatings, and then the rigors of weather when, having escaped, he crossed desert regions and mountains on foot and under cover of night. His body also withstood days on end of interrogation and the "chair-lift," an instrument that gradually forces the legs towards the hands which have been bound behind the back—an instrument still in use in the Congo, where it outraged the good-hearted westerners who happened upon photographs of it in their newspapers. And Emilio Uriondo had other qualities too: he was studious, self-taught, and had a political grounding like few others, although he was not one to parade it: he was very well read in the theses of Bakunin, Marx, Kropotkin, Engels, Malatesta, and Lenin. However his belief was that without action theory served no purpose, which is why the campaigns of the anarchist intellectuals who professed to be scandalized by a Di Giovanni or a Roscigna failed to impress him.

This Uriondo was the person Roscigna needed to mount his forthcoming coup, but Uriondo was in prison. So he had to look for a replacement. He needed men of action and there were few of those. He chose to take on the Moretti brothers, two men whose beliefs were unclear but who had risked their lives more than once. They had spearheaded a strike against the oil company, La Energina. The strike had arisen out of the "expropriation" of fuel by the tanker drivers. The company had discovered this and sacked them, whereupon anarchist solidarity was manifested in a very violent dispute, which even sparked controversy within the libertarian movement. At that point, Eliseo Rodríguez, a Spanish anarchist of unimpeachable record, entered the story. More of him later.

Roscigna now had his men about him: Andrés Vázquez Paredes, Vicente Moretti, and Antonio Moretti, all of them ready to follow him anywhere.

On October 1, 1927, at the entrance of Rowson Hospital, mingling with people coming and going, and patients and their associates, there were three men with bandaged heads. Accident victims, no doubt. They hung around the doorway there, as if waiting for somebody, and nobody paid any attention to them. In fact, they actually were waiting for someone: the messenger whose job it was to deliver the wages and who was almost due.

The three bandage-headed men were Miguel Arcángel Roscigna, Andrés Vázquez Paredes, and Antonio Moretti. Thirty meters away, Vicente Moretti was waiting at the wheel of a Phaeton.

Roscigna realized that the job was a tricky one. He had discovered that the police officer escorting the messenger was a former champion marksman, which is why the raiders were relying heavily on the element of surprise. Roscigna hated "drama," all this shooting for its own sake and the needless bloodshed.

When the messenger stepped out of the car with the briefcase in his hand, the trio approached and threatened him with their handguns. Suddenly everything went pear shaped. The briefcase was dropped, one of the anarchists gathered it up and made a run for the car. The other two followed, but one of them, when he turned around, spotted the policeman drawing his weapon. Instinctively, he fired first and his shot struck home. As he ran on, he saw the policeman collapse.

The newspapers would later make it known that this was Francisco Gatto, a Buenos Aires policeman and that he was, to all intents and purposes, dead the moment he was shot.

The proceeds of the action were considerable: 141,000 pesos, but before they could think about how to put it to use, they had to flee because, in spite of several false leads, the police were hot on their heels. A great pal of Yrigoyen's, and an old enemy of the anarchists, Inspector Santiago, headed the investigation. From the outset, he sensed that this was the work of anarchists. The driver Dositeo Freijo Carballedo was the first to be picked up. He was the scapegoat in the investigation. Whenever a bomb went off or there was a hold-up, this Spaniard was always the first to be pulled in for questioning. He was certainly no saint, but he had nothing to do with this job.

Roscigna realized that the time had come to leave Buenos Aires and slip into Uruguay where he had some very good friends. To this end, he called upon the services of the Andalusian Bustos Duarte, a boatman on the Tigre River and an unconditional supporter of the anarchists. It was he who, some months later, would harbor Severino Di Giovanni in the delta, when the police were hot on his trail.

Bustos Duarte was ready. Roscigna and the Moretti brothers were to sail with him aboard the *E pur si muove*. Vázquez Paredes was to follow another itinerary. They would leave the car in a garage in San Fernando, recommended by a neighbor, known to one and all as "Bébé Castro." The three fugitives crossed the delta and spent the night at a ranch belonging to Don Hilario Castro (Bébé's father) in Palmira.

But the San Fernando garage owner was a man who played both sides of the street. After receiving a handsome sum for hiding the car, he reported them to the police.

The entire leadership of the detective bureau and the Social Order sprang into action immediately. They raced to the garage, found the getaway car there, arrested Bébé Castro, and burst into the home of the boatman Bustos Duarte. He was not home but his wife was, and taken by surprise, she gave full and frank answers to all of the police's questions. She identified photographs of Roscigna, both Morettis, and Vázquez Paredes who, she added, had not made the trip on her husband's boat.

For the Argentinian police, it was an open and shut case. So they sought cooperation from the Uruguayan police and sent several delegations to Colonia, Palmira, Carmela, and Montevideo. All available resources were mobilized to apprehend those responsible for the Rawson Hospital raid. Meanwhile, Roscigna and the Morettis, after having circumnavigated Palmira on horseback, rented a car and set off for Montevideo. They were relying on help from the *baqueano*[18] Osores, a Uruguayan ready to risk his neck for the anarchists.

Comments made to the press by the Argentinian inspectors Santiago and Zavala filled all who were awaiting the three anarchists' capture with optimism. They were on their heels, and there were hourly bulletins on the progress of the chase. From Palmira, they went to La Agraciada via Drabble, travelling north. Arriving in Soriano, they pressed on to Mercedes, where they took the Montevideo road. They spent the night in Cardona in a little hotel right across the street from the police station. Witnesses came forward from everywhere they'd been, and it was all detailed in the press. For example, *La Prensa* related how, in Cardona, the runaways had put in some shooting practice in a place known as La Lata. As it stated in its October 16 issue that year: "Roscigna is regarded as the ringleader of the malefactors and the supposition is that he wields great moral sway over his accomplices, due to his daring and determined nature, and his gifts as a redoubtable sharpshooter, as proved during a display before a number of people in La Lata (in Cardona). Thirty meters from them, and using a Winchester rifle, a Mauser rifle, and a revolver, he managed to

---

18   *Baqueano* from *baquía*, meaning practical knowledge of a region's roads, tracks, trails, and rivers: a *baqueano* would be an expert guide.

shoot holes in a coin no bigger than a Uruguayan peso coin. Roscigna regarded this exercise as both practicc in a technique that might prove useful to him at any moment and as a demonstration of his absolute mastery of the 'sport'."

They left San José barely minutes ahead of the Uruguayan police, briefed in detail by the Argentinian police. Eventually they arrived in Montevideo and started off with a drink in the "De Salvo" café on the Millán and Vilardebó avenues, and bade the *baqueano* Osores farewell. They walked from the café to the barber's near the vegetable market on José L. Terra Street for a shave. They disappeared down the streets of the workers' districts where numerous anarchists lived. And there the trail petered out; the police could discover nothing further, despite all their efforts. All the optimism evaporated. And then the press began to take the police severely to task for their slowness. *Crítica* availed of the chance to make sarcastic remarks about Inspector Santiago's men. Every page carried a headline like, "Throughout Uruguay and all the way here the police discover phantom vehicles." One box in the newspaper, headlined "A Tale in the Style of Mark Twain," read:

Mark Twain has regaled us with the grotesque adventures of these detectives, with their magnifying glasses, following the trail of a runaway elephant. Absorbed by their quest, noses pressed to the ground, they scrutinize the imprints left among the very many others by the feet of the fabulous pachyderm. Suddenly they blunder into an unexpected bulk. Whereupon they raise their eyes and find themselves nose to nose with the elephant which the have only just sighted, a few millimeters ahead, in spite of his monumental size, and almost accidentally. That is exactly what is happening to our police—the world's best. In their efforts to see better, they can see nothing, and when they can see something, it is because others let themselves be discovered. If there were any doubt as to the theoretical efficiency of our detectives, it would be dispelled by their infallible hypotheses. But once on the ground, one vexatious detail, one wasted minute, any error of timing, space, or distance puts a bewildering distance between these expert sleuths and their quarry. The finest music-hall entertainment certainly could not have dreamed up scarier and more comical situations than those offered to us on a daily basis by the world's finest police force in the most spectacular of investigations.

The newspaper *Crítica* had raked in the profits from its edition given over to the Rawson Hospital raid and to detailed descriptions of the pursuit of the fugitives into Uruguay; its circulation was climbing steadily and people could not get enough of its news. One could even have imagined that the paper was on the fugitives' side, but obviously that was far from the truth. Roscigna was well aware of this: he had a fine grasp of the methods of the sensational press. Basically *Crítica* kept the police on the alert. The four anarchists would rather that nobody talked about them than that they should be front page news every day in the best-selling newspaper, not to mention on its inside pages, complete with drawings of them. But Roscigna was not a man easily riled. Had it been Di Giovanni, for instance, he would have gone in person to the editors, defying all risks, and ordered the editor in chief to cease his campaign on the pain of taking four bullets for his trouble. But Roscigna was to make maximum capital out of the coverage in *Crítica*. He sent in several letters, which Botana [the publisher] reprinted in each edition. These letters—a play that Vázquez Paredes would utilize later on—were peppered with clues, place names, and imaginary witnesses that only baffled the police more.

The days went by and Santiago, Zavala, Gariboto, and all their sleuths had to admit defeat and go home. It only remained for them to wait and to trust in that irreplaceable police weapon: informers, persons to be found in every walk of life: servants, porters, news vendors, drivers, office workers, lawyers, doctors, servicemen's parents, sacristans, the devoutly religious, prostitutes, and pimps. This whole spectrum of free collaborators was the most effective "fifth column" that the police deployed to defeat anarchist activism.

Few events of the day had so captured the public's imagination as did the Rawson Hospital raid and the hunt for Roscigna and his comrades. In Uruguay, the matter was raised in Parliament and the Interior minister was asked to make a report after the failure of the Uruguayan police's efforts. In Argentina, *La Prensa* reproached people for their lack of civic courage, in that, while the raid was in progress "nobody took the risk of intervening, neither to prevent the raid nor to assist in the arrest of the offenders."

Of course, given its profile, the episode made an impact within the anarchist movement, too. *La Protesta*, under Abad de Santillán's by-line, distanced itself from the incident and from "the Roscignas and Morettis" and urged anarchists "to call to a halt and to isolate this source of perversion and deviation of our ideas and methods of struggle: regrettably, anarcho-banditry is a real plague." By contrast, *La Antorcha*, the paper run by González Pacheco, wrote that the whole thing was a police concoction and that neither Roscigna, Vázquez Paredes, nor the Morettis had any hand in the Rawson Hospital raid.

If González Pacheco was to be believed, the whole affair was just "a sinister reactionary plot, a framing job by the police against militant anarchism."

There is a sinister motive in this, and behind it all, there is an equally sinister personality: Inspector Santiago. Inured to a life of infamy, this new instigator of persecution and violence directed at anarchism reckons that he can play his last card against us in this way. He is deluding himself: by resorting to such methods he won't succeed in severing the ties between the laboring classes and a movement that springs from them and represents, at present, the only hope for the world. What neither violence nor terror nor death have been able to defeat cannot be defeated by a police conspiracy that is both sinister and ham-fisted.

Then, in a plain retort to the men around *La Protesta*, this same González Pacheco stated his position on the anarcho-bandits:

> These offenders, are they good or bad? What difference should that make to us, comrades? That question, which should be put to a judge, but never is, should be glossed over by ourselves and left to be consumed by the roaring flames of our vengeance: they are victims. Without lapsing into sentimentality about those who erect illegality into a system, we may assert that they are always better than those who repress them. You want examples by which to evaluate them? If we could offer only one, it would be this: the criminal is more of a human being than the beat cop who is himself less of a cur than his inspector who remains less of a beast than his superior who is never quite the riff-raff that the president of the Republic or the monarch at the head of the kingdom is. Who embodies power embodies evil. The others are mere links in a chain that ends in a ring that garrotes the poor wretch who has fallen to greater depths. The latter,

chained to his life of misery, pays the price of the
orgy of blood and tears from which the others
drink. He is the victim not only of the penalty
inflicted upon him by perverts, but also of these
"honest men" who still believe in legality. That is
the palinode that we should be singing to criminals. Every puritan—even if he professes to be an
anarchist—is, in his heart of hearts, a legalist, just
as any woman who prides herself on her chastity
of soul is, in her heart of hearts, a bourgeois. Like
the capital of the bourgeois, her capital of virtue is
built on the misfortunes of her sisters. The criminal is a man stripped of his alleged honor, the
prostitute a woman stripped of her supposedly
virtuous love. Faced with them, an anarchist can
never speculate about whether they may be good
or bad: he can only sweep them up into his fight
against the bourgeois and bourgeoisies. Taking it
on board, taking it all on board. Less law-abiding
virtue. More anarchist militancy.

As well as to meet the needs of solidarity with the
cause, Roscigna used the proceeds from the Rawson
Hospital raid to fund the making of counterfeit money.
Anarchist expropriators operating in Argentina had a
deadly fixation with counterfeiting money. Roscigna
was convinced that he could beat the bourgeoisie with
the help of counterfeit currency. To that end, he was relying upon a fairytale figure, the German Erwin Polke, an
unprecedented expert in the art of forgery. Polke was a

taciturn sort—an individualist anarchist, an avid reader of the theoretician Max Stirner—and a loner who only sprang to life when it was suggested to him that he should counterfeit money. He never asked anyone for a helping hand. He lived frugally and lived like a recluse. The only thing he ever got out of life was imprisonment, and he served time in prison for what remains an offense nonpareil: within the very precincts of the Punta Carretas prison in Montevideo, he manufactured counterfeit Argentinian currency of outstandingly high quality. To do so, he was dependent on a rather skillful and preposterous disciple: Fernando Gabrielsky.

But the matter of counterfeiting currency is an issue separate from the violent expropriation we are discussing here. Let us say merely that Roscigna had to spend some time in Montevideo. He knew that going back to Buenos Aires meant that the death penalty awaited him on every street corner. The Argentinian police were going to take revenge however they could for their failure to capture Durruti, for the killing of officer Gatto at the Rawson Hospital, and for the shame of the failed chase from Palmira to Montevideo.

Emilio Uriondo, who was charged with planting a bomb at the United States Embassy in Montevideo, was released on February 11, 1926. Roscigna and Uriondo would be resolute in their opposition to the plan drawn up by the Moretti brothers and three Catalan anarchists:

A few months before the Rawson Hospital raid, Antonio and Vicente Moretti had their wives and children move to Montevideo and settled them into the maid's quarters at a house in Rousseau Street in Villa de la Unión. There, they lived humbly, making ends meet as street vendors of neckties.

As for the three Catalans, they were young men from Durruti's group. He had advised them to get out of Spain where they had been heavily "involved." They were eligible for the death penalty. They had been behind upwards of a hundred bomb attacks in Barcelona and were wanted by the military police for conducting anarchist propaganda inside the prisons; for seriously injuring a general, two colonels, and several officers; and for escaping from military custody. Their names were Tadeo Peña, Pedro Boadas Rivas, and Agustín García Capdevilla,[19] and they came to Roscigna with "references" from Durruti. They had been charged with passing on a "special" invitation from Durruti, who was asking him to come to Europe because he had need of a man of action. Roscigna declined. He asked Durruti to forgive him, but the struggle in Argentina was preoccupying him too much for him to contemplate leaving.

The three Catalans were hotheads eager for action:

---

19   These three mavericks' favorite pastime was to accost the first officer they met in the street, threaten him with guns, take off his cap and toss it into the middle of the street, then have him take off his boots, which they also threw into the middle of the street. Finally, they would force him to take of his trousers in front of the stunned onlookers who could only flee the scene. Once reduced to this embarrassing condition, a few shots between the legs would send the officer packing.

the weapons they were carrying were burning a hole in their pockets, and they could not "wait," as Roscigna had urged. In Roscigna's estimation, an "expropriation" operation on Argentine soil should be deferred. Calm had returned there and it was better to do one's best to assist the runaways out of Argentina. In addition, the campaign to secure the release of Simón Radowitzky—a campaign that was meeting with significant popular backing—was at its height and, that being the case, anarchists should not be implicated in incidents that might well cost the campaign popularity.

But the Morettis and the three Spaniards acted independently and carried out a raid that resulted in a bloodbath and led to a tragic end for Roscigna.

The hold-up of the Messina bureau de change was mounted "in Bonnot Gang style." The aim was not just to grab the money but also to throw the bourgeois into panic with an outright act of terror. They stepped inside shooting in all directions and covered their retreat by shooting at anything that moved. The upshot was that they carried off 4,000 Uruguayan pesos but left three people dead and another three wounded. The dead were the bureau's manager, Carmelo Gorga, a well-known Uruguayan horse-racing aficionado; his clerk, Dedeo; and the taxi driver, Fernández, who refused to drive the raiders. The incident created a great sensation because it had happened within meters of the governor's home.

In the course of the raid, the three Catalans had let slip a few words in their native tongue and the

Uruguayan police deduced from that that the Durruti-Ascaso-Jover group was still in operation. Seeking confirmation, they asked the French authorities for further background details, but they also carried out numerous swoops on anarchists, because this time, the police simply had to do something: the entire press was clamoring for action. The brains behind the investigation was the renowned Inspector Pardeiro, who enjoyed the same standing as Velar in Rosario, or as Habiage in Avellaneda, because he used methods that were soon associated with the name of Leopoldo Lugones (junior) and were to be dubbed "the Bazán law."

Thanks to an informant, Pardeiro found out that the robbers had gone to hide out in the maid's quarters in a house at 41 Rousseau Street, in Villa de la Unión. And the information was spot on. At 4:00 a.m. on Friday November 9, 1928—that is, two weeks after the hold up—three hundred men from the Uruguayan army and police, armed with submachine guns and rifles and backed by fifty firemen with all sorts of ladders, stood by to storm the premises. They cut off the power supply and set up searchlights. The preparations were so thorough that, when the inhabitants awoke, they were greeted by the sight of at least ten heads at every window and guns trained on them.

Inside the house were Antonio and Vicente Moretti and the three Catalans, as well as Pura Ruiz and Dolores Rom, the Morettis' wives, plus two very young children. Seeing that any attempt to resist would mean certain death for their families too, the anarchists surrendered. But before coming out, Antonio Moretti made a desperate decision. He would not give himself up: he raised his hands, brought his gun up to his right temple, and took his own life. He had previously told his brother that the police would never take him alive.

Inspector Pardeiro, congratulated in person by the Buenos Aires police chief (Yrigoyen's supporter, Graneros), did all that was humanly possible to get Vicente Moretti to betray Roscigna's whereabouts. But Moretti, though he was under a greater strain following his brother's suicide, knew how to keep his mouth shut. This is taken from his statement: "It is true that I know Roscigna, but I have not seen him for some time. He had no hand in the Rawson raid, nor in the Messina job." He added that all that he knew was that "Roscigna lived a respectable life for eight months in a Malvin beach-house."

The owner of the Rousseau Street house, however, claimed to have seen Roscigna go in two nights before and speak with the Morettis and the Catalans, which tended to suggest that the man Pardeiro was most interested in was still in Montevideo. And so the hunt continued. Roscigna now had his back to the wall; he had nowhere safe to turn. While Emilio Uriondo headed for Brazil, Roscigna returned to Argentina.

In the end, they both decided to come back in order to "spring" their arrested comrades from Punta Carretas prison in Montevideo, but to carry out such a difficult operation they needed lots of money. And they were ready to get hold of it by the only means available to people on the run: "violent expropriation." Roscigna kept his word and laid the preparations for springing the prisoners from Punta Carretas. As in any operation by anarchists, it had something far-fetched and unlikely about it, like some funny story, some romantic adventure.

Meanwhile, back in Argentina, some very important anarchist expropriator groups went into relentless action over a short but intensive period of time. These were truly violent times, especially the last year of the Alvear government, the two years of Yrigoyen's rule, the Uriburu years, and Justo's years. Everyone who had been pointing out that violent anarchism had emerged as a result of Yrigoyen's passivity came to appreciate that they had been mistaken. Indeed, under the Uriburu government and in spite of executions and ferocious repression, the anarchists continued to take to the streets, to gamble with their lives, plunge deeper and deeper into the impasse, and watch as they lost their comrades one by one.

Roscigna was involved in the February 1929 raid on the Kloeckner plant, and in October 1930, with Uriburu's repression at its height, he joined Severino Di Giovanni in an attack on the Sanitary Services wages clerk in Palermo. Seventy percent of the booty from that, which stood at 286,000 pesos, was set aside for helping anarchist prisoners. Miguel Arcángel Roscigna and José Manuel Paz (a Spanish anarchist known to his colleagues as "The Captain") took a goodly sum off to Montevideo to finance an undertaking that was already under way.

Indeed, in August 1929, a couple of Italians—and their little daughter—left Buenos Aires to settle in Montevideo. They purported to be business people and they bought a plot of land in Solano García Street, facing the Punta Carretas prison. The police immediately ran a check on their identity, because they kept a close eye on the prison's neighbors. Everything seemed to be in order: the newcomer's name was Gino Gatti and he planned to open a coal yard. Within a short time he had built a sort of hangar complete with living quarters and put up a sign reading "'El buen trato' coal depot: charcoal and coal sales." The Gattis were very pleasant to all their customers. Señor Gatti was very polite and won over his neighbors. Every day the couple could be seen driving off in their car, which had been purchased from the previous coalman, Benjamín Dominici, to deliver bags of coal.

But in the first week of March 1931, the neighbors found that the Gattis had decided to give up on the business—even though it was booming—and go back to Argentina. Everyone was sorry to see them go, and Gatti the coal merchant said his goodbyes, flashing his usual friendly grin. The days passed.

On the afternoon of March 18, a prison warden from Punta Carretas was keeping a watchful eye on the prisoners who were enjoying their fifteen-minute stroll in the prison yard. He sensed that there was something awry, but couldn't tell what. He had received formal instructions to keep a particular eye on the German Erwin Polke, but Polke was blithely playing chess in the middle of the yard. Maybe that was what was out of the ordinary. In fact, one might even think that Polke had settled down right there in order to draw the attention of the wardens down upon himself.

Within a few minutes, shouting, whistle blasts, and sirens echoed outside the prison. The shouting came from some neighbors of the "El buen trato" (Good Deal) coal yard who had spotted strangers coming out of the back yard and thought they were robbers about to rob the Gattis' erstwhile depot. Police and wardens quickly cordoned off the depot, at which point two people were spotted trying to escape by the rear door. Finding themselves surrounded, the pair retreated back inside, but by then it was too late. They were quickly apprehended.

What a surprise it was for the wardens to recognize two of their inmates, one of them Antonio Moretti's brother-in-law, Aurelio Rom. On searching the coal depot, the police met with a further surprise: they came upon a well, lighted to perfection and so deep that it seemed to plunge down to the center of the earth. It was two meters by two meters and lined with boards. One could climb down four meters into it by means of a little ladder. There, a tunnel fifty meters long led from it. "It's a perfect job, technically speaking," the police experts later conceded. A person of average height could walk through with ease. With its arched roof, it had electric light and ventilation from the outside. Every twenty meters, there was a bell for signaling back to the entry point. And the exit from the tunnel was worked out to perfection. It was next to the toilets of the prison block that held the anarchists.

Of course, the construction of the tunnel had been the work of Gino Gatti, henceforth dubbed "The Engineer," and also of Miguel Arcángel Roscigna, Andrés Vázquez Paredes, "Captain" Paz, and Fernando Malvicini (an anarchist from Rosario who was a member of Severino Di Giovanni's group until two months before Di Giovanni was executed in La Penitenciaria).

On the night before the escape attempt, they stopped work fifty centimeters from the toilet block in the prison: that was the final phase of their task. They had dug away the walls and had shored them up with a carjack. On the day of the escape, during recreation time, Roscigna and his comrades had used that same jack to lift the paving stones in the toilets. Vicente Moretti, his brother-in-law, and the three Catalan anarchists imprisoned since the raid on the Messina Agency were the only inmates in the know. Moretti was the first to stroll over to the toilets where he found the hole and the little ladder leading down. The three Catalans followed after, ahead of five ordinary prisoners who grabbed the chance to make a break for it. Nine of them in all. Aurelio Rom and another ordinary prisoner were caught while preparing to slip out.

There were three cars waiting for the escapees in the street behind the rear yard of the coal depot. There they made their getaway and left no trace.

Roscigna had kept his pledge to spring his comrades. But the escape, carried out with perfect timing and without a single shot being fired, would result in Miguel Arcángel Roscigna's own capture.

Vicente Salvador Moretti was at large for only nine days. The worst thing was that his liberators were captured with him.

After spending the night at the home of the anarchist Germinal Reveira, at 2326 Legionarios Street, Moretti and the three Catalan anarchists split up, going in different directions. Roscigna was waiting for Moretti in a hideout that he thought was safe: a house in Curupí Street, near Flores Avenue, opposite the Maroñas racetrack. The committee of the Uruguayan Radical Colorado party was based in the apartment at street level, and the house's owner, Roberto Dassore, had leased the ground floor back room to Roscigna and Moretti. It was an ideal place for coming and going, because there were always plenty of people around and it enabled them to pass unnoticed.

Every morning, Roscigna stepped out to buy a newspaper. He delighted in chatting with people on the street. Lest he attract attention, he had changed his suit for humbler garments: a striped jacket and some cheap trousers, some espadrilles and a cap. Just as he was paying for his newspaper, Roscigna indulged himself in some banter with the newsagent.

"Let me have one of those bourgeois rags that talks about the raiders," he said, and lingered for a chat. The manner in which he had requested the newspaper attracted the attention of the vendor, who, without hesitating, reported it to the local inspector. The next day the inspector dispatched two detectives to the corner to take a look, but Roscigna failed to show up that day because something else had happened before the newsagent reported him.

In fact, on March 27, 1931, a dogcatcher's van was roaming around Curupi Street: it was nothing more than a car topped with a cage packed with uncollared dogs. The dogcatcher, who used a lasso to catch the strays, was an ex-convict: José Sosa, a pimp and pickpocket who had served several months in Punto Carretas. Outside the Radical Colorado party offices there was a wretched mongrel that refused to let itself be caught and sought refuge within the building. Sosa followed it inside. Vicente Moretti was having a cup of Paraguay tea and savoring the coolness of the morning on the patio. Sosa's unexpected arrival startled Moretti at first. He shouted, "Leave the doggie alone, mate!" Sosa made a show of protesting and left empty handed, but very pleased with himself. He had just recognized Moretti, the escapee from Punta Carretas, whom he knew very well, having been in the same prison block as him. At that point, he left the van and the dogs and ran to the police station. Breathlessly, he announced: "I've seen Moretti, there… It's him… I know him well!"

Uruguayans are given to preparing for any eventuality. They even marshaled the 4th cavalry regiment of the Uruguayan army for the storming of the house on Curupí Street. But there was no need. As they entered the house, gripping their rifles, the fifty-three officers came upon Moretti absorbed in his reading out on the patio, blissfully unaware of what was going on. At that very instant, Roscigna emerged from his room. He was unarmed and saw the others training their guns on him. Caught off guard, he failed to act.

The moment of capture is something that anarchists on the run from the police habitually discussed with each other. And Roscigna often told his comrades of the divergent reactions of two Russian anarchists upon the scaffold: the peasant Gabriel Michailoff and the student Rissakoff, the two authors of the attempt on the life of Alexander, tsar of all the Russias. Michailoff was a twenty-one-year-old peasant, as strong as a bear, with long hair and lively bright blue eyes. They took him to Simeon Square to hang in front of all the villagers. In front of the unspeaking men and women who had turned out to watch the spectacle—some had even brought their children along—the hangman raised the noose to slip it around his neck. The bear-like Michailoff, utterly calm, raised his head and stretched out his neck accommodatingly. But something unbelievable occurred: just as the hangman was springing the trapdoor and as the peasant's heavy body was dangling mid-air, the rope snapped and Michailoff fell to the ground. He struggled to his feet, his neck half dislocated and almost broken, bruised and bloody at the same time. Then, with the same dignity, he offered his neck to a second noose. But this one, assuredly too thin for somebody of Michailoff's bulk, also snapped like a thread. The child of the steppes made a superhuman effort to get to his feet, but this time he remained on all fours, blinded by the blood that swamped his eyes. His breathing now only a rasping noise, because of the bubbles filling his lungs. It took eight soldiers, peasants' sons like Michailoff himself, to drag him up as best they could. And, on tiptoe, they hung a third rope around his neck. This time the rope got the better of him and didn't give way beneath the weight of his body, which was jerking around like a headless chicken.

But the crowning glory of the spectacle was to come from the student, Rissakoff. He was fetched, well bound with ropes that seemed to have cut off the blood supply to his long hands, so white did they appear. He was completely ashen and his face told the story of Russia's poor starving students. He did not proffer his neck as Michailoff had. Quite the opposite. He put up some desperate resistance and went on the attack. He had only his teeth to defend himself, and he began to dance around almost comically like a madman, trying to bite the hands of all the prison guards straining to cling on to him. He was like a wolf at bay, defending himself against a pack of dogs. This went on until one policeman, shrewder than the rest, delivered the coup de grace: he grabbed Rissakoff by the hair while a colleague grabbed his feet, and they brought him to the ground while kicking him. They turned him over and then straightened him up panting for breath like a cockroach with a broken back. Some people insisted that, right up to his final breath, Rissakoff was still snapping at them.

Roscigna, empty-handed, had their guns trained on him. Was it worth his while putting up pointless resistance like Rissakoff had? That's what Severino Di Giovanni had done two months before. Or should he, like Michailoff, proffer his neck with dignity and surrender? He opted for the latter course. He knew that in any event he was to be handed over to the Argentinian police. Vázquez Paredes, Malvicini, and "Captain" Paz were captured at the same time.

The Uruguayan newspapers trumpeted Roscigna's capture. Not knowing how to play up their accomplishment, the police put all four of them—Roscigna, "Captain" Paz, Malvicini, and Moretti—on display in the station courtyard, sitting on chairs with their hands bound behind their backs.

All the pressmen from both banks of the River Plate turned out to view the anarchists. They removed the spectacles from shortsighted Roscigna. He responded curtly and with dignity to the reporters' questions. He became more talkative when he turned with profound scorn to the police. He stated that they were the "poorly paid lackeys of the exploiters and bureaucrats in power."

To explain what he had done with his life, he declared that "One day the anarchists and their methods will get the credit they deserve: we are financed by no one, whereas the police are in the pay of the State, the Church has its own funds, and the Communists are subsidized by a foreign power. That is why, in order to make revolution, we should rely only upon the means we find in the streets at the risk of our lives."

The extradition request emanating from the Argentinian Foreign Affairs ministry arrived with stunning rapidity within hours of news getting out that Roscigna had been arrested. Inspector Fernández Bazán had rushed the procedure through. Moreover, the Interior minister, Don Matías Sánchez Sorondo, who had responded with alacrity, and who could scarcely have been mistaken for a sympathizer with the Radicals or with Yrigoyen's supporters, had a visceral distaste for anarchists.

Fernández Bazán, with his practical approach to things, knew that individuals like Roscigna were beyond redemption. It was a waste of time putting them in prison: even under lock and key, they would always be a danger. Drastic problems called for drastic solutions. Let Di Giovanni be the precedent: four bullets and it was all over. Several years would pass before a second Di Giovanni would be born. In the interim, there would be peace.

For his part, Roscigna knew that he was in a very tricky position. If extradition was granted, he would be handed over, bound hand and foot, to the Uriburu dictatorship, which would have him shot out of hand, if indeed he ever made it to the dockside. He was familiar with the procedure: they took delivery of a prisoner in accordance with all the legal niceties and then, five meters further on, "the individual attempted to resist by seizing one of the guards' weapons, whereupon it was necessary to shoot him down."

Roscigna knew that while his hands were steady at the moment of action, the same was true of Fernández Bazán. The anarchist thought it over and came up with a solution: he denounced himself to the Uruguayans as the man behind the escape of prisoners from Punta Carretas and for having stolen three cars to help them get away. Malvicini, "Captain" Paz, and Vázquez Paredes did the same. For as long as the trial lasted, they could not be returned to Argentina. The Uruguayan courts sentenced them to six years in prison each. They had successfully extended their lifespan by that, but no more. Fernández Bazán would not be denied.

As we have seen, expropriator anarchism in Argentina threw up very special figures with very singular characters. The most outstanding personalities in the movement were doubtless Severino Di Giovanni, Miguel Arcángel Roscigna, Buenaventura Durruti, Andrés Vázquez Paredes, Emilio Uriondo, Juan del Piano, Eliseo Rodríguez, Juan Antonio Morán, Gabriel Argüelles, Gino Gatti, and lots of others. We will not sit in judgment on whether their actions were well- or ill-founded. The society in which we are living has already done that.

During that short decade of violence during which they were active, the expropriator anarchists were progressively sucked into an increasingly narrow vicious circle. Today their fight looks like a pointless effort, a needless sacrifice. Their violence served more to assist in their own destruction than to bring about the success of their ideals. They carried out armed raids and counterfeited money to meet their movement's needs, secure the release of their prisoners, and look after the families of fugitives. But in those actions, more than one would find himself going behind bars (if not killed): the ones who were left were in turn sucked into the same deadly spiral and so on and so on. With but few exceptions, virtually none of them made any personal gain from what was "expropriated," contrary to what both the police reports and the accounts of the "intellectual" anarchists or the pure syndicalists of their day may have claimed. Those who were not killed and who managed to survive the prison regime in Ushuaia returned to their old trades as bricklayers, textile workers, or mechanics, toiling hour after painful hour in spite of their years. To put it another way, we may question their ideal and the methods for which they opted, but we cannot question their attachment to that ideal, which they embraced through thick and thin.

Within this ever-narrowing circle of activities, what they termed "vendetta" gradually came to assume a capital significance. The expropriator anarchists pursued vengeance against their natural enemies: the police. Thus, they eliminated Inspector Pardeiro with a bullet in the head in an attentat that left the whole of Montevideo rattled (that operation, determined by Miguel Arcángel Roscigna, was carried out by Armando Guidot and Bruno Antonelli Dellabell).

With a rifle shot they disfigured for life the renowned "Basque," Inspector Velar, a specialist in the hunting down of anarchists (that operation was planned by Severino Di Giovanni and Miguel Arcángel Roscigna, and carried out by Roscigna and Paulino Scarfó—the anarchists say—or by Di Giovanni and Scarfó—according to the actual victim).

Those two were the most famous of a series of score-settlings with the police. The most spectacular one, though, was the attack on the army Major José Rosasco, appointed by President Uriburu "operational police chief of Avellaneda," following the "revolution" of September 6, 1930, which overthrew Yrigoyen.

"Sánchez Sorondo, Leopoldo Lugones (junior), and Rosasco are the three members of the revolution who bought it." That was the unanimous comment of the young conservatives who savored Mussolinian vocabulary. They had been expecting something quite different from the September coup d'état, which had started so well, by pushing aside the sniveling Radicals, thanks to the boys from the Military Academy. But there it stopped, half way, with the country not rid entirely of its Radicals, anarchists, and other vermin. Which is why men like Rosasco were needed if a reality was to be made of what Leopoldo Lugones (senior), the poet of the revolution who eulogized the nation, the nation's strength, and the nation's violence, had been clamoring for. Lugones (senior) would accept "decent foreigners" who had entered his country in search of work but not "foreigners who strike in support of a foreigner [as in the case of the strike in support of Radowitzky] on national soil."

So Lieutenant General Uriburu knew what he was doing when he awarded Major Rosasco the title of "operational police chief of Avellaneda." Avellaneda was in fact a quintessentially industrialized, working-class area where the anarchists were a force to be reckoned with. Hence the strikes and hence all our ills! Uriburu had asked Rosasco to clean up Avellaneda as a matter of urgency.

Major Rosasco arrived in Avellaneda and had two petty thieves shot, after ordering them tied to a bench. They were crying for their mother. He attended the execution in person, not being the sort to let himself be deterred by the sight of blood. When the bloodied boys slumped forward, he rubbed his hands as if to rub off this carrion which had no right to life, before moving on to other business.

Rosasco had not come to cleanse Avellaneda of the fleshpots reserved for the conservative district bosses. No, simply to mop up the trade union side. And there he was not inactive. When Rosasco had had his shower, pulled on his trousers and his gleaming boots, and donned his jacket with its major's insignia and his cap, he cast a quick glance at the mirror and ventured out: "Tremble, anarchists!" He mounted impressive dragnet operations. The Black Marias would stack up at the door of the Avellaneda police headquarters. Persons arrested were treated harshly, for they were always rebels: Spaniards,

Catalans, Italians, Poles, Bulgars, and even a bunch of Germans who had formed a vegetarian society, which struck him as suspect.

Every time a bomb went off in Avellaneda, there was another round up. And when Rosasco wanted them to sing, sing they did. He used methods that never failed.

In Avellaneda, there were no judges or lawyers worth a damn. The interests of the Nation took precedence over the Constitution and over what liberals call individual guarantees. A foreign anarchist falling into Rosasco's hands would never tread Argentinian soil again—Rosasco sent him to Sánchez Sorondo who implemented Law 4144, the residence law. And an Argentinian anarchist who fell into his hands was shipped directly to Ushuaia. And, of course, Rosasco always had the death penalty introduced by the September revolutionaries: he could execute anybody who resisted, anybody caught red-handed.

But this apostle of force and violence would find himself out on the pavement facing someone for whom violence held no fears. His name was Juan Antonio Morán and he was a steersman. He was a true *criollo* from Rosario, but he was, above all else and from the top of his head down to the soles of his feet, an anarchist.

Juan Antonio Morán presents an unblemished figure. Along with Uriondo, he gives the lie to the allegation that activist anarchism in Argentina was the creation of foreigners alone. Moran had twice been general secretary of the Maritime Workers' Federation, which was probably the mightiest labor organization of the day. He led the dock strikes, which were characterized by extreme violence.

He was the very model of an activist anarchist leader. He was not to be numbered among these leaders who make do with issuing appeals through the press: when a strike was on, then strike it was, and he could stomach neither non-strikers nor scabs. He was not the sort to send out strike pickets while he remained ensconced in the union headquarters. Quite the opposite. Out he would go with his gun to roam the port. The moment they saw him approach, the dockers who were not wont to obey orders, immediately ceased work. And if they failed to come ashore, Morán would clear them off the ships himself. One day, he spotted a scab working, perched on a ship from La Boca. Morán drew his gun, aimed it just above his head and fired. That argument was sufficiently convincing for the scab to come ashore and vanish at a run.

On October 12, 1928, Morán found himself implicated in a very serious matter. A strike had been declared, and the Mihanovich Company stopped at nothing in its attempt to defeat the Maritime Workers' Federation. It hired "free labor," which was guarded by squads from Carlés's Patriotic League and by assault troops, many of them brought in from Paraguay. In the port, every hour brought fresh incidents. That particular afternoon, Juan Antonio Morán was at the union headquarters when two dockers arrived to warn him that the Mihanovich men were in Pedro's bar at the corner of Mendoza and Brandsen streets. There were more than thirty of them and the Paraguayans Luciano Colman and Pablo Bogado led them. And Colman had just announced: "We're here looking for Morán. We're going to settle his hash."

Morán said nothing as he listened to the dockers' tale and he did not respond. A few seconds later, he made for the door and spoke a few words with the police officer posted there to monitor all the comings and goings. The moment the officer turned his back, Moran slipped out unseen, and within minutes he was in the bar where the Mihanovich men were gathered. He strode right up to Colman and told him:

"I know you've been looking all over for me to kill me. Well, I'm Morán. I'm the guy you're after!" Whereupon a gunfight ensued. Upwards of thirty shots were fired. When the din died away, the men hiding underneath the tables and behind the counter lifted their heads: Colman lay dead and Bogado was seriously wounded.

When the policeman charged with keeping the union premises under surveillance heard the gunfire, he raced to the scene of the shooting. Morán slipped back to the headquarters unseen and resumed his work. Bogado, the wounded one, accused Morán of having slain Colman. The police went to fetch him and placed him under arrest. But the prosecution could not come up with a single witness and was obliged to set him free after a few months.

Himself a man of action, Morán sought out other men of action within the anarchist movement. Thus he made the acquaintance of Severino Di Giovanni, Roscigna, and all who were wanted in connection with "expropriation" operations. This trade union leader, who spent days chairing meetings or in negotiations with bosses' representatives, sought out his friends in the evenings. And he saw nothing odd about planning armed raids or bomb outrages and then going and carrying these out. Who could have dreamed that the seamen's leader would have had this other side to him? "He was extremely daring, determined, and capable of tackling any situation, no matter how difficult," *La Nación* wrote of him a short time later.

Even as Major Rosasco was starting to decimate the Avellaneda anarchists, lashing out also at the Radicals along the way, Morán realized that the only answer was to call in the "expropriators."

In this instance, there were no messages, no protests, no recourse to lawyers or writs of habeas corpus. In Avellaneda, Major Rosasco's approach prevailed. On his side, the major had the State, with its whole panoply of repression, and society, the fear of an entire people who, falteringly, had begun to march in step.

To confront all that, there was an increasingly tiny band of men bereft of their main leaders—of Severino Di Giovanni (shot), Paulino Scarfó (shot), Miguel Arcángel Roscigna (imprisoned), Andrés Vázquez Paredes (imprisoned), Emilio Uriondo (imprisoned), Eliseo Rodríguez (imprisoned), Silvio Astolfi (gravely wounded), Juan Márquez (slain), Braulio Rojas (slain), and we could carry on with the endless list of those who had been rendered out of action.

Morán decided to "take on" Rosasco.

In this contest, the only factor in the anarchists' favor could be the element of surprise. The expropriators acceded to Morán's proposal. Julio Prina, a philosophy student, would come down from La Plata. "Bébé" Lacunza would also be at Morán's side. The only son of a peasant from San Pedro, he'd had his baptism of fire alongside Severino Di Giovanni and Emilio Uriondo in the raid on La Central Bus Company. The third man to accompany Moran as his driver was a Spaniard, González, whose picturesque life was to peak in 1944 when he entered a liberated Paris aboard a tank belonging to the Leclerc Division. Finally, he had backing from "The Engineer," one of the most intriguing members of the group. Though personally opposed to violence—because he believed the bourgeoisie could be fought using other more ingenious methods—"The Engineer," when invited by his comrades, was up for any of the most dangerous and risky operations.

On the evening of June 12, 1931, Major Rosasco, accompanied by the deputy mayor of Avellaneda, Eloy Prieto, left police headquarters to go to dinner in the "Checchin" restaurant 150 meters away. Rosasco was very happy, having just rounded up forty-four anarchists, including some youths who had been distributing leaflets that read: "Death to Rosasco!" To tell the truth, those kids were about to lose their taste for printing, even if they were only printing "Little Red Riding Hood"!

Rosasco had summoned the press to announce that he had thwarted yet another anarchist plot.

They stepped inside the restaurant and ordered their first course, which they wolfed down with a good appetite. Once the first course was finished, "five respectably dressed individuals" climbed out of a car. One of them sat at a table beside the door, and the other four walked to the back of the dining room, as if making their way to the yard.

Some wisecrack had just drawn gales of laughter from Major Rosasco when, all of a sudden, the four individuals stooped down in front of his table. One of them stepped forward. He had the look of a *criollo* about him and seemed as strong as an ox. He moved towards Rosasco and shouted at him: "Dirty pig!" Rosasco stood up slowly, his eyes bulging. The stranger, who was none other than Juan Antonio Morán, drew, equally slowly, a Colt .45 and fired five shots, all of them deadly.

The five men then took to their heels and, to cover them, Julio Prina fired some more shots that inflicted slight injuries upon a young man and Prieto.

At this point, the drama reached its second act: as he fled, one of the anarchists stumbled and crashed through a plate glass window. By then, his colleagues were back in the car waiting for him: they thought it must just be a slight accident, but this wasn't the case. The young man—Lacunza—never got up again. He was dead. The anarchists quickly retraced their steps to retrieve their comrade's body. They managed to bundle it into the car, and raced off.

There are two stories about how Lacunza died. The first says that he had been hit by a shot fired by Prina, having unfortunately been in the line of fire. Our preference is for the second story: Lacunza suffered a heart attack during the assassination and dropped dead. The absence of any trace of blood at the scene of his collapse and on the route leading to the car bears out this latter version.

Major Rosasco's funeral was an impressive one.[20] It amounted to a veritable display of the dictatorship's might. The highest authorities from army and navy

---

20   This was an anarchists' leaflet printed in Montevideo and smuggled into Buenos Aires on June 11, 1931:

> ROSASCO!
>
>   The executioner of the regime that is oppressing and degrading Argentina, the right arm of the government's barbarism, which sows tears, terror, shame, and grief among the proletarian families of Avellaneda, the sadistic torturer of social and political prisoners, has been executed. At last. Only Uriburu and his crew, the dictatorship's mercenaries and lackeys, the hypocrites and the cowards, will weep for Rosasco. He was a brute in human form who paraded his stripes and trailed behind him a sword thirsty for proletarian blood.
>
>   Anarchist consciousness, ever inflexible in the presence of executioners, has singled him out and sentenced him to death. Servitors of their ideals and prepared for sacrifice, spokesmen for the libertarian passions of an Argentina in chains, these proletarian fighters have shown, by executing Rosasco, how we may be rid of the dictatorship, root and branch.
>
>   —THE ANARCHISTS

attended, and all available flights of air force planes at Palomar overflew the cortage.

The Church sent along its entire hierarchy: the "Country Society,"[21] Jockey Club, and Military Circle[22] all sent emotional delegations. Groups closely associated with Catholic nationalism and the elite of Buenos Aires, Avellaneda, and La Plata were also represented at it.

The assassination was a gauntlet flung down by the subversive anarchists in front of the government, army, and police. And the police in charge of inquiries would enjoy carte blanche: woe betide the anarchist that fell into the hands of the authorities just then! The first one they came upon in the course of a search was gunned down without a trial. He was Vicente Savaresse, a member of Tamayo Gavilán's group. And he'd had nothing to do with Rosasco's assassination.

The police never did manage to find out who killed Rosasco, though they always suspected the steersman Juan Antonio Morán. He was, moreover, sentenced to death in absentia.

What we have published here for the very first time is the actual story of how Major Rosasco was assassinated and the names and persons involved. Nearly forty years have passed and the killing is now part of history. The author has had to chase up many lines of inquiry in order to reveal what has until now been a real mystery. Historical truth requires that today

---

21   The Sociedad Rural was the big landowners' association.
22   The Officers' Club.

we say who bore the responsibility for an act that they looked upon as an act of justice.

On May 2, 1931, the police managed to trace one of the anarchists for whom they had long been searching: Silvio Astolfi, a great pal of the late Severino Di Giovanni. Astolfi was a tiny Italian with very fair hair, a devil-may-care sort, who took life as it came. But when it came to shooting, he was a fearsome gunman. He had taken part in a hundred operations, always with that same indifferent attitude. But on May 2, the situation was a lot more serious for this Italian. He had just recently joined the group of Tamayo Gavilán and that very day had helped it rob the wages delivery from Villalonga at the junction of Balcarce and Belgrano streets. The number of shots fired had characterized that raid, like all of Tamayo's raids. Once they had the money in their grasp, the anarchists fled down Balcarce Street. Silvio Astolfi was behind the wheel; he loved high-speed driving.

At the junction of Mexico and Balcarce streets, a policeman, alerted by the sound of gunfire, opened fire at the raiders' car and managed to inflict a fatal wound upon eighteen-year-old Mornan, who was on his first robbery and was sitting in the back seat. Silvio Astolfi was also struck in the head, but he didn't let go of the steering wheel, despite the blood pouring over his forehead and down his face. They fled as far as the intersection of Villafañe and Ruy Díaz de Guzmán streets, where they came to a halt, having run out of gas. They all got out of the car. Astolfi was unsteady on his feet;

his clothing was saturated with blood. The Chilean, Tamayo Gavilán, made to accompany him but Astolfi told him: "Save yourself. My goose is cooked." He sat down on a doorstep, then stood up again and made his way down Villafañe Street as far as Azara Street. It was then that a policeman named Máximo Gómez found him. Astolfi stuck out his tongue at him and started to run with all the strength he could muster. A hellish chase began. Astolfi darted down Villafañe Street as far as Diamante Street, then on to Ruy Díaz Street. Despite all the shots fired by the policeman, Astolfi fired only one, in an effort to make his ammunition last. Slipping down Ruy Díaz Street, he arrived at Martín García Street where he spotted a passing tram. He leapt on to the forward platform and thus arrived at the intersection of Caseros and Bolívar streets, where he jumped into a taxi. He threatened the driver and forced him to drive down Caseros Street to Tacuarí Street. From there, he cut down Martín García Street and got out at No. 669, where there was a foundry. Even as he was getting out he saw officer Gómez hot on his heels. Astolfi ducked behind the jamb of a metal portal and rested his gun on his left arm to take aim at the policeman, who spun around and was hit in the buttocks by Astolfi's bullet. Our exhausted anarchist then seized his chance to wipe away the blood that was blinding him before carrying on his long journey. This time he went down Martín García Street and reached España Street in the middle of the crowded Barracas district. The inhabitants were startled to see this devilish lad race past.

At the end of España Street, he turned into Uspallata Street. The bloodiest chapter of this marathon began where Uspallata meets Montes de Oca Street.

In Uspallata Street, sergeants Fernández and Montes, and officer Martínez cut off Astolfi and fired a hail of shots at him.

Astolfi ran back up Montes de Oca Street, making for Ituzaingo Street, zigzagging because he was almost out of ammunition. Panting for breath, he was limping along but spotted another taxi approaching. He stopped it and threatened this driver too. He tried to shake off his three pursuers but they too got into a car and followed him, sparking off a further fusillade during which at least thirty shots where fired, one of which hit the taxi's rear tire. Astolfi got out in Pablo Giorello Lane, but there another policeman awaited him and tried to stop him by firing over his head. Astolfi stopped for a moment and took aim. The policeman was hit in the head and killed instantly. Astolfi realized that the lane was a dead end and that he had to find a way out right away. Now there were four people chasing him, including police officer Tranquilo Perna, who fired over his head. Astolfi played his last card. As he fired the last bullets, he capitalized on the confusion to reach the middle of the street. A cab pulled up and the driver said, "Get in quickly, Comrade Astolfi!" This was a member of the Drivers' Union, who, as luck would have it, just happened to be passing. They raced away at top speed, and though chased by a police car from the 16th precinct, managed to disappear.

Astolfi was driven to the home of Benedicta Sette-case de Montaña, then on to that of Nicola Recchi, who in turn smuggled him into Gino Gatti's hide-out. Gatti drove him out to La Plata where Dr. Delachaux, a friend to anarchists, tended to his very grave injuries. Within a few months, he was restored to health. After that odyssey around Buenos Aires, he was driven to Montevideo and then went on to Barcelona, where he joined up with Durruti.

In spite of the repression and their casualties, the anarchist expropriator movement was still showing signs of strength in 1932 and 1933, mainly in La Plata, in Avellaneda, and in the capital, Buenos Aires.

In La Plata, they could count on the constant and unstinting assistance of Antonio Papaleo, whose home was always open to fugitives.

Armed raids and attempts to break people out of prison were carried on at the same pace. One of the prisoners, Eliseo Rodríguez, pulled off a partic-ularly daring escape from a cell in the basement of La Plata police headquarters itself. Pedro Espelocín escaped from the hospital where he was being held under guard. Rodríguez rejected suggestions that he should cross into Uruguay and opted instead to stay behind to help a comrade break out. Along with Espe-locín he joined up with the group of Juan del Piano, Gino Gatti, and Armando Guidot. Juan del Piano was a baker's boy with a strong personality. He had two passions: anarchism and trying to get the best possible care for his son who had been paralyzed from birth.

Meanwhile, the Prina brothers from La Plata (Julio and Toni) were active with Juan Antonio Morán, Daniel Ramón Molina (who worked at the docks), Julio Tarragona, Ángel Maure, Pedro Blanco, and Victor Muñoz Recio. These were two small groups but they fought to the bitter end.

At the end of 1932, at the instigation of Rafael Laverello and with help from Morán, Prina, Molina, and Gatti, a new tunnel was dug. This time it started from an apartment near the jail, and it was designed to secure the release of Emilio Uriondo and other anarchists. It was even better thought out than the Punta Carretas tunnel. It was fifty-eight meters long and went right up to the prison laundry. But after they had dug the first twenty-three meters, they had to call it off because the police were closely watching all of the men involved. And besides that, they were starting to run out of money.

Then came a series of blows dealt by the unrelenting Inspector Bazán. On January 19, 1933, Tarragona and Molina were killed after they shot two police officers in the Aldo Bonzi district. On March 16, in Rosario, Pedro Espelocín was killed, and Eliseo Rodríguez and Armando Guidot were arrested. The following day, the police captured Gino Gatti in Córdoba.

Around the same time, the Prina brothers fled to Spain. On June 28, a police squad cordoned off a house in Mitre Avenue in Avellaneda and caught Juan Antonio Morán asleep. That left just one: Juan del Piano. The police knew that he was hiding out among farmers south of Santa Fe. There, near Firmat, on August 11, 1933, he managed to hold out until his last bullet was gone and the police killed him.

It was all over now. There was no one to work for the freedom of those in jail, which is why, on October 7, 1933, the anarchist prisoners in Caseros made a desperate attempt. Little by little they had explosives, grenades, and handguns smuggled in from the outside. They blew up a wall and tried to force a way out to the street. The break started at 6:30 p.m., Mario Cortucci (a member of the Di Giovanni group) and Ramón Pereyra (from Tamayo Gavilán's group) led the way, and Gino Gatti and Álvaro Correa Do Nascimento (a Brazilian anarchist) brought up the rear. They passed through the bars and down a corridor while a hellish hail of gunfire raged. Arriving at last in the outer courtyard, Cortucci was hit in the head and killed. Pereyra detonated a grenade, which blew off his left hand. The prison guards regrouped and fired all over the place, while training their spotlights on them. At that point, the 3rd Cavalry Regiment arrived and took up position facing the prison, setting up their machine guns. The anarchists could not advance and they retreated to their block until the gunfire stopped. Their escape attempt had failed. The guards had lost three men, one anarchist had died, and another was seriously injured. But for the survivors the consequences of the desperate operation would prove fatal. Most of them would wind up in Ushuaia.

By the start of 1935, the country was calm, but Fernández Bazán was not resting on his laurels. He knew that Juan Antonio Morán and Miguel Arcángel Roscigna were still alive and still dangerous, even behind prison bars. Morán was in Caseros and Roscigna in Montevideo.

At the beginning of May that year, the courts decided to free Juan Antonio Morán for lack of evidence, but something rather odd happened before that. On several occasions, Morán had been fetched from his cell and paraded past a number of persons unknown who had looked him over at some length. These were plain-clothed police.

On May 10, Morán learned that he was due for immediate discharge. His fellow prisoners advised him to not to leave the prison before being in touch with a lawyer, but Morán neglected the advice. He signed his discharge papers—and effectively signed his own death warrant. The prison gates opened. Morán took a deep breath. He had taken barely two steps before he was grabbed brutally by the neck, and then by his arms and legs and bundled into a car that raced from the scene.

Two days later, a shepherd came across a man's corpse on a track near General Pacheco. He had been shot just once, in the back of the head, but his body had been severely mutilated. It was no easy task to identify the body, but it was indeed Juan Antonio Morán, anarchist. He had been subjected to the sort of torture subsequently practiced on a grander scale by the murderous commandos of the Triple A (Argentine Anti-Communist Alliance) under the Peronist government in 1974 and 1975.

His funeral was an occasion for a demonstration of the workers' wrath. Speakers cried "Vengeance" as their fists punched the air.

On December 31, 1936, Miguel Arcángel Roscigna, Andrés Vázquez Paredes, Fernando Malvicini, and "Captain" Paz completed their prison sentences.

That date was circled in Inspector Fernández Bazán's diary. Everything was in place.

A police delegation under the command of the Social Order commander Morano had traveled to Montevideo. Uruguay had turned down an extradition application but there was an unspoken arrangement between the two police forces. Classified under the law as "undesirables" in Montevideo, they were to be deported to Buenos Aires. But right there at the docks in the Uruguayan capital, the "packages" were handed over, well and truly bound, to Morano's team. During the river crossing, they were not allowed to budge, and they were taken straight from the port to the Central Police Department. Judges La Marque and González Gowland, who were handling the charges arising out of the Rawson Hospital and La Central armed raids, arrived to conduct the questioning at the Department, because they were being held there. Then, for lack of evidence, Roscigna, Vázquez Paredes, and Malvicini were released and their final journey began. "Captain" Paz was transferred to Córdoba, where there were other charges still outstanding against him. He was freed shortly after by some armed comrades who rescued him from the police station.

When Donato Antonio Rizzo, secretary of the Prisoners' Defense Committee, and Roscigna's sister called at the police station to ask where the three anarchists were, an official told them that they had been transferred to La Plata. In La Plata they were told that they were in Avellaneda. In Avellaneda, that they were in Rosario. In Rosario, that they were in the station at Tandil. And so on. Such was the calvary of Roscigna's sister who clung to hope of seeing her beloved brother alive, but all in vain. One day, though, hope flared again: a fisherman from Maciel Island had seen three handcuffed men bound for the southern dock precinct unloaded from the rear of a Black Maria. Roscigna was leading the way. The journalist Apolinario Barrera, from *Crítica*, was promptly alerted and the headline, "Roscigna in South Dock," was carried full-page size.

It looks as if this was a signal to Fernández Bazán that the prisoners in transit had to be finished off. From that moment on, no trace was ever found of the three anarchist militants. Efforts continued however: even the Barcelona libertarian groups sent money for the inquiries to be continued. It was virtually certain that they had been murdered, but people clung to a last shred of hope anyway. Up until that day, several months after they had disappeared, when an official from Social Order confided to the men from the Prisoners' Defense Committee and told them privately, "Don't wear yourselves out, lads. Roscigna, Vázquez Paredes, and Malvicini were on the receiving end of the Bazán law. They were dumped at the bottom of the River Plate."

To this day, this macabre episode has never been clarified. The bodies have never been recovered, and the truth will never be known. Roscigna, Vázquez Paredes, and Malvicini were the first three of the "disappeared" victims of Argentinian state terrorism. The military would apply the very same methods thousands of times under the Videla dictatorship.

Juan Domingo Perón rewarded Inspector Fernández Bazán for services rendered by appointing him deputy chief of the Federal Police in 1947, and then transferred him to a diplomatic career, which according to Bazán, had always been his "true calling."

With the "*revolución libertadora*,"[23] he would retire and spend his final years in solitude. Before his death, he asked to have his remains cremated, just like so many of the anarchists he fought. Fernández Bazán was the only Peronist official, who, after he died, would receive a tribute in *La Prensa*, above Gaina Paz's byline. His obituary was also fulsome in its praises of the "Bazán law."

We have now reached the end of this bitter chapter in our society's life. Illegalist anarchism was of course an option in those days because of the desperate conditions of the time. Violence against violence; justice for all rather than the prevailing social injustice. Are we, then, making the case for the anarchist expropriators? No! We are content simply to relate the facts. Was there justification for their extreme response? As

---

23   The "liberating revolution" was the coup d'état that unseated Péron in 1955.

we see it, any answer to that question must be subjective. There are white-collar workers and bureaucrats who spend their whole lives countenancing injustices, and there are people so primed for rebellion that the slightest abuse of power provokes them to react. There are those who march in step and wear a uniform, and there are others who accept no other constraints than those rooted in logic, which is not always compatible with human nature. These two outlooks were to be found in the dramatic conflicts of the rural society at the turn of the century. There was the *peón*, submissive and cowering from the cudgel of the boss, and there was that other one who, at the first lash of the whip, drew his knife, wrought justice and became an outlaw.

We have just recounted the sordid and epic tale of men who opted for a difficult and heroic solitary path and followed it to its bitter end, to its abrupt and final conclusion. History was not on their side because the solutions for which society seeks can never be reached by such lonely by-ways.

Appendix:

A Note on Severino Di Giovanni[1]

Further details of Severino Di Giovanni's life can be found in Osvaldo Bayer's essay *The Influence of Italian Immigration on the Argentinean Anarchist Movement*:

> Among the Italian exiles reaching Argentina were pro-organization anarchists (such as Luigi Fabbri and Ugo Fedeli, who lived there for a time before settling in Montevideo) and some individualists. Among the latter there was one group

---

1   This appendix was added as a note to the French edition, published on-line at: http://basseintensite.internetdown.org/IMG/pdf/anarexpropriateurs.pdf.

that demonstrated that they were ready to resort to equally radical methods in order to combat the radicalization of the regime back in the home country. The most determined of these was Severino Di Giovanni, who was born in Chieti in 1901. In Buenos Aires, he embarked upon a period of violence that might be regarded as the nearest forerunner of the urban guerrilla war that was to proliferate on a much greater scale—albeit flying different ideological colors—in the Argentina of the 1970s…

The dizzying spiral of violence started almost innocently on June 6, 1925. That day, Buenos Aires's Italian colony was celebrating the twenty-fifth anniversary of the accession to the Italian throne of Victor Emmanuel III. The festivities culminated at the Colón (Columbus) Theatre, in the presence of the Argentinean president, Marcelo T. De Alvear, and Italian ambassador, Luigi Aldrovandi Marescotti, the Count Viano. When the orchestra struck up the Italian national anthem, a noisy incident erupted: a gang of anarchists, Severino Di Giovanni among them, disrupted the occasion by scattering leaflets and chanting: *Death to fascism!* That was the start of it. They were all members of the *L'Avvenire* group except for Di Giovanni, who belonged to the *Renzo Novatore* circle and was publisher of the magazine *Culmine*.

Some days after that, in connection with the campaign on behalf of Sacco and Vanzetti, the group around Di Giovanni embarked upon a bombing campaign targeting premises belonging to US firms, as well as the US Embassy. Di Giovanni remained closely linked to the New York-based *L'Adunata dei Refrattari* paper and with groups that followed the line of the Italian individualist Luigi Galleani , a school of thought to which Vanzetti belonged. The flurry of violent acts in Buenos Aires and Rosario would culminate in high explosive bombs going off at Italy's consulate-general, entirely demolishing it, claiming the lives of nine people, and seriously injuring another thirty-four. Those attacks and bank raids galore triggered an indiscriminate political crackdown on Italian and domestic anarchists. This was why *La Protesta*, the leading Argentinean anarchist newspaper, and the FORA labor confederation, openly attacked the gang of Italian individualists over these incidents. Relations became so strained that Severino Di Giovanni would put several bullets into and kill *La Protesta*'s managing editor, López Arango, after the paper dismissed him as a "fascist agent."[2] There was no truth to any of these accusations.

Domenico Tarizzo's book *L'Anarchie* (Seghers, 1979) offers some additional detail:

---

2   The actual author of that epithet was Diego Abad de Santillán. Several years later, he spread around that Di Giovanni had been a communist agent posted to Argentina by Palmiro Togliatti. See Santillán's *Memorias: 1897–1936* (Barcelona: Planeta, 1977), 212.

Di Giovanni was born into a very poor family. An intellectual and worker, he was working as a typesetter when the fascists came to power, and in 1923 he immigrated to Argentina. In Buenos Aires, he both wrote and published the anarchist paper, *Culmine*, which carried a column titled "Face to Face with the Enemy" and cataloged attacks. [In 1926] he orchestrated a massive demonstration calling for the release of Sacco and Vanzetti. He was arrested there for a bomb attack on the US embassy, only to be freed for lack of evidence. This brought him into contact with two brothers of Italian extraction, Alejandro and Paulino Scarfó, with whom he would take part in underground activity. [In August 1927, when the news broke that Sacco and Vanzetti had been executed,] two bombs exploded in Buenos Aires: one at the Washington monument, one at a Ford dealership. The US ambassador placed an insertion in the press, arguing that Sacco and Vanzetti had been common criminals. In the light of that provocation, those anarchists supporting violent action (notably Di Giovanni and the Scarfó brothers) retaliated with a string of attacks. The police blamed Di Giovanni for them all. That November, a manufacturer, whose strong point was not good taste, launched a new brand of cigarettes, "Sacco and Vanzetti." His name was Gurevich, and a bomb made him halt production immediately. On Christmas Day, the National City Bank was blown up. Two of its

American and Argentinean customers were killed and another twenty-three injured. On May 3, Di Giovanni bombed the Italian consulate, the bugbear of antifascists and anarchists; nine people died and thirty-four were hurt. Shortly after that, the anarchists blew up a pharmacy belonging to a well-known fascist, Beniamino Mastronardi, and, on February 1, 1931, the home of Colonel Afeltra, a notorious torturer of antifascists in Italy. Severino Di Giovanni was shot, captured following a shoot-out with the police. The following day, Paulino Scarfó was shot; in order to share his comrade's fate, Scarfó confessed to all of the hold-ups carried out by the group. Di Giovanni had met Durruti who had taught him his bank hold-up technique. In 1930, he reprinted the works of Elisée Reclus in a very polished edition. That very year, General Uriburu seized power and set about shooting down anarchists.

Index

A

Álvarez, Manuel, 56

Abad de Santillán, Diego, 4, 7, 12-13, 26, 57, 62, 75, 80, 137*n*; expropriator critique, 94

Afeltra, Colonel, house bombing, 139

Aguzzi, Aldo, 72

AK Press, 2

Aldrovandi Marescotti, Luigi, 136

Alfonso XIII, assassination attempt, 77

Alvarez de Toledo, Ambassador, 70, 76

Alvear, Marcelo T. De, 136 regime of, 69, 72-3, 76, 77, 102, 136

Anarchism and Violence, 2

Anarchism: Argentine expropriation movement, 3; Argentine internationalism, 7; Argentine intra-violence, 5; historiography, 1; illegalist, 133; 'pragmatic', 29; -syndicalism relation, 4

Antonelli Dellabell, Bruno, 113

Aráuz, Jacinta, 51-2

Arango López, 4, 75; killing of, 5, 21, 137

Argentina: early 20th century repression, 4; -France extradition diplomacy, 76-7; France debt to, 70; judges,

40, 131; Law 4144, 116; martial law, 23; *revolución libertadora* 1955, 133; Social Order Department, 64, 81; state terrorism, 133; USA embassy bombing, 138

Argentine Patriotic League, 17-18, 37-8, 41, 44, 49-51, 53, 74, 117

Argentine Union of Trade Unions, 55

Argüelles, Gabriel, 112

Armand, Émile, 57

Armeñanzas, Modesto, 47

Ascaso, Alejandro,(aka José Pontón), 67-8

Ascaso, Francisco (aka, José Cotelo/Pichardo Ramos), 13, 20, 68-71, 73; extradition issue, 75-6; Paris release, 78

Astolfi, Silvio, 119, 124-7

Avellaneda district, Buenos Aires, 115-16, 120, 123, 127

Avrich, Paul, 2

B

Babby, Andrei (Juan Konovesuk), 32-4, 40-2; life sentence, 43

Badaraco, Horacio, 82

Bakunin, Mikhail, 51, 57, 86

Bandera Roja, 29

Barcelona: May Days 1937, 13; Police of, 66

Barreiro, Doctor, governor Misiones province, 35-6

Barrera, Apolinario, 132

Bayer, Osvaldo, 1-6, 9, 12

Bazán, Fernando, 70 111-12, 128-9, 131, 133; 'law' of, 83, 100, 132

Bernard, Francisco Morrogh, 50

Blanco, Pedro, 128

Boadas Rivas, Pedro (Pere), 10, 21-2, 98

Bogado, Pedro, 118

Bolshevik revolution, Russia, 4, 28-9, 81; expropriators critique, 26; turn against, 46

Braintree hold-up, USA, 58

Bustos Duarte, 88-9

C

Canovi brothers, 51

Caplán brothers, 34

Carcano Caballero, Ramón (Durruti alias), 64

Carlés, Manuel, 38, 41, 44, 49, 50, 74, 117

Carrasco, Buenos Aires police, 70

Cascros prison, Buenos Aires, 12, 83, 130; escape attempt, 23, 129

Castro, Hilario, 89
'Chair lift', torture technique, 86
Chelli, Luis, 35, 39, 42
Civic Guard, 38
Colman, Luciano, 118
Comite Pro Presos y Deportados, 9
Congo, 'chair lift' use, 86
conspiracy charge, use of, 43
Correa Do Nacimento, Álvaro, 129
Cortucci, Mario, 129
Costa, Prosecutor, 42
counterfeiting money, 96-7
'Country Society', 123
Crítica, 41, 92-3, 132
criollos, 85, 116
Culmine, 19-20, 75, 136, 138

D

Dassore, Roberto, 106
De Alvear, Marcelo T., (*see Alvear*)
Del Piano, Juan, 112, 127-8; police killing of, 23, 129
Di Giovanni, Severino, 3, 5-8, 19, 21, 47, 59, 72, 75, 80-3, 86, 89, 93, 102, 105, 110-12, 114, 119-20, 124, 135-9; execution of, 22
direct action, advocates of, 46
dock strike 1921, 49

Domecq García, 41
Dominici, Benjamin, 103
Dreyfus, Alfred, 57
Drivers Union, 126; fascist attack on HQ, 51
Durruti, Buenaventura, (aka Arévalo Salvador/ Ramón Caballero), 4,, 13, 20, 60-2, 64, 68-9, 71, 73-4, 77, 79, 84, 98, 112, 127, 139; -Ascaso-Jover group, 100; extradition issue, 75-6; Paris release, 78

E

Eighteen Months of Military Terror, 23
El Internacional, 47
El Libertario, 29
Elephant Editions, 2
Engels, F., 86
Espelocín, Pedro, 53; escape of, 127
'expropriation': anarchist ideological conflict, 46; expropriators self-defense origins, 49
expropriations/raids: Bank of Chile, Santiago 1925, 8, 19, 63-4, 66-7; Bank of Gijón, Spain, 67; Buenos Aires customs post 1921, 47; Chacarita district 1919, 27;

Kloeckner plant 1929, 102; La Central Bus Company, 120, 132; Las Heras tram depot 1925, 19, 62-3, 66; Messina Bureau de Change 1928, 10, 21, 99, 101, 105; National City Bank bombing, 138; Perazzos, 30-3; Primera Junta, 19, 64, 66; Rawson hospital, 20, 79, 87-8, 92, 94, 96-7, 101, 131; Rio Negro mail coach 1923, 56; San Martín Bank, 19, 65, 68, 79; Sanitary Service clerk Palermo, 102; Villalonga wages snatch, 124

F

Falcón, Ramón, killings by and of, 16
Fabbri, Luigi, 57, 135
Fedeli, Ugo, 135
First of May 1909, 4
Fishman, Bill, 2
Foppiano, Police Inspector, 35
FORA (Argentine Regional Workers' Federation), 7, 9, 72*n*, 137; 5th Congress, 15, 55; *La Antorcha* boycott, 19; 9th Congress split, 16; Tenth Congress, 1928, 21

France: -Argentina extradition diplomacy, 72-8; pro-anarchist prisoner campaign, 71
Freijo Carballedo, Dositeo, 88
Frías, Daniel J., 43
Frías, Jorge H., 43

G

Gabastou, Mariano, 41
Gabrielsky, Fernando, 97
García Capdevilla, Augustín, 98
Gariboto, policeman, 93
Gath and Chaves company, 40
Gatti, Gino, (aka 'The Engineer') 22, 80, 103-5, 112, 120, 127, 129
Gatto, Francisco, 88, 97
Geneva, 37
Gómez, Andrés, 56
Gómez, Máximo, 125
González Gowland, Judge, 131
González Pacheco, Rodolfo, 48, 94-5
González Roura, Octavio, 43
Gorga, Carmelo, 99
Gori, Pietro, 57
Grondona, Alfredo, 41
Gualeguaychú, farmworker-landowner clash, 50

Guidot, Armando, 113, 127
Gurevich company,
    bombing, 138

H

Hernando, Esteban, 56
'Hunt Down the Russians',
    Argentine fascist slogan,
    38

I

informers, 93
International Red Aid, 76
Italian Anti-Fascist
    Committee, 47, 81
Italian Consulate Argentina,
    bombing of, 139
IWMA (international
    Workingmen's
    Association), 7

J

Jockey Club, 41, 123
Joll, James, 59, 61
Jover Cortés, Gregorio, (aka
    Lúis Victorio Repetto/
    Serrano García), 20,
    67-9, 71, 73; extradition
    issue 75-6; Paris release,
    78
Justo, regime of, 102

K

Karaschin, anarchist

comrade, 27
Kronstadt, Bolshevik
    repression, 81
Kropotkin, P., 86

L

L'Adunata dei Refrattari, 8,
    59, 137
L'Avvenire, 136
La Antorcha, 7, 23; 52, 56,
    70, 72, 75, 78, 82, 94;
    'direct action' advocacy,
    46; expropriators
    support, 13; FORA
    boycott, 19; FORA
    expulsion, 9; ideologues
    of, 54; -*La Protesta*
    anatagonism, 6; 1932
    publication cessation,
    74; "Robbers" editorial,
    48; start of, 18; Viedma
    prisoners campaign, 56
La Chacarita, revolutionary
    committee attempted, 38
La Energina company strike,
    86
La Marque, Judge, 131
La Nación, 119
La Penitenciaria Nacional,
    Buenos Aires, 42, 83
La Plata astronomical
    observatory, Buenos
    Aires, 34
La Plata police HQ escape,
    127

La Prensa, 35, 50, 60, 64, 90, 94, 133

La Protesta, 5, 7, 11, 15, 29, 35, 46, 50, 52, 55-6, 94, 137; expropriation denouncing, 8, 75; gunmen of, 18; ideologues of, 54; -la Antorcha anatgonism, 6, 18; printing press destroyed, 16

La Razón, Argentine Patriotic League paper, 37, 41

Labrada Pontón, José Manuel (Alejandro Ascaso alias), 64

Lacunza, "Bebe", 120-1; death of, 122

Lanciotti, Umberto, 81

landowners, militias of, 49

Laverello, Rafael, 128

Leclerc Division, Liberation of Paris, 120

Lenin, V.I., 29, 36, 46, 86

Leval, Gaston, 7

Los Solidarios, 8, 10-11, 19

Lucich, Pérez Millán assassin, 45

Lugones, Leopoldo (junior), 74, 100, 114

Lugones, Leopoldo (senior), 114

M

Márquez, Juan, 120

Malatesta, E., 57, 86

Malvicini, Fernando, 110, 112, 131; 'disappeared', 133; presumed murder of, 132

Maritime Workers' Federation, 9, 117

Martínez, Police Officer, 126

Martin, James J., 1

Marx, K., 86

Mastronardi, Beniamino, business bombed, 139

Matrichenko, Juan, 34

Matteotti affair, 58n

Maure, Ángel, 128

Maximalist revolution, Petrograd, 27

Michailoff, Gabriel, 108-9

Mihanovich Company, strike at, 117

Military Academy, 114

Military Circle, 123

Molina, Daniel Ramón, 128

Montevideo, 90-1, 103

Morán, Juan Antonio, 3, 9-11, 13, 22, 112, 116-21, 123, 128; torture and murder of, 12, 23, 130

Morano, Social Order commander, 131

Moretti, Antonio, 86-7, 89-90, 94, 97, 99, 100, 104; suicide of, 101

Moretti, Vincente Salvador,

86-7, 89-90, 94, 07, 99-101, 105-8
Muñoz Recio, Victor, 128
Mussolini, Benito, 58*n*

N

'The Nameless Ones', 10
Newton, Eduardo, 43
Novatore, Renzo, 136

O

Organization for the Defense of Property, 49
Osores, *baqueano* [guide], 90

P

Papaleo, Antonio, 127
Pardeiro, Police Inspector, 100, 113
Paris, 37
Pampa Libre, intra-Anarchist attack on, 18
Patagonia, farm laborers strike, 49;
Patagonia Rebalde, 2
Patiño marshes, 37
Patriotic League, *see Argentine Patriotic League*
Paz, Gaina, 133
Paz, José Manuel ('The Captain'), 102, 105, 110, 112, 131
Peña, Tadeo, 98

Perazzo, Pedro A., 29; *see also* expropriations
Perazzo, Señora, 34
Pereyra, Ramón, 129
Pérez Millán, 44-5
Perna, Tranquilo, 126
Perón, Juan Domingo, 133
Pichardo Ramos, Teodoro, 64
Police, score-settling with, 113-4
political prisoners: campaigns for, 52-3, 54; support for, 83; solidarity collections, 84
Polke, Erwin, 96-7, 104
Prieto, Eloy, 120-1
Primo de Rivera, dictatorship, 67
Prina, Julio, 120, 121, 128
Prina, Toni, 128
Prisoners' Defense Committee, 132
Proudhon, P.-J., 57
Punta Carretas prison, Montevideo, 85, 97, 101-4, 107, 128; escape from, 105, 112

R

Radowitzky, Simón, 16, 27, 55, 73, 77, 79, 85, 99; release of 21
Ramos Mejía, Francisco, 43
Rawson Hospital, see also

expropriations

Recchi, Nicola, 81, 127

Reclus, Elisée, 57, 139

Reveira, Germinal, 106

Rissakoff, 108-10

Rizzo, Donato Antonio, 132

Rodríguez, Eliseo, 87, 112, 119, 127

Rojas, Braulio, 120

Rom, Aurelio, 104

Rom, Dolores, 100

Romanoff, anarchist comrade, 27

Romero, Buenos Aires policeman, 70

Rosasco, Major José, 114-16, 119-20; assassination of, 10, 22, 121; funeral of, 122-3

Roscigna, Miguel Arcangel, 3-4, 8-9, 13, 19-24, 47, 54-5, 79-84, 86-102, 105-8, 110, 112-4, 119, 130-1; 'disappeared', 133; arrest of, 111; presumed murder of, 132

Ruggerone, Casiano, 56

Ruiz, Pura, 100

Ruiz, Rafael, 66

Russell, Francis, 59

Russian labor circles, Argentina, 37

Russian, -Jewish, fascist identifying, 38

Russian Revolution 1905, failure of, 37

Russian Revolution 1917, see Bolshevik revolution, Maximalist revolution, 81

S

Sacco, Nicola, 7-8, 59

Sacco and Vanzetti, case of, 71, 73, 79, 82; support campaign, 9, 57-9, 76, 136-8

San Ignacio, Misiones province, 34

Sánchez Sorondo, Matías, 111, 114, 116

Santa Fe province, 37

Santiago de Chile, 64

Santiago, Police Inspector, 88, 91

Santillán, Policeman, 42-3

Savaresse, Vicente, 123

Scarfó, Alejandro, 138

Scarfó Paulino, 22, 114, 119, 138, 139

Sears, Hal, 2

Seeber, Ricardo, 43

Serrano Garcia (Gregorio Jover alias), 64

Silveyra, Ramón, prison escape of, 55

Simon Radowitzky and People's Justice, 2

Social Defense Law 1910, 4

Social Prisoners and

Deportees Defense Committee, 54-5, 72, 76

Socialist Congress, Geneva 1904, 36

Soldevila, Cardinal, Zaragoza assassination, 67

Sosa, José, 107

Spain: Civil War, 61; -France non-extradition, 70

Stirner, Max, 97

strikes: docks 1921, 49; General 1909, 16; La Energina, 86; Mihanovich company, 117; Patagonia farm labourers, 49; Vasena 1918, 16-17

T

Tamayo Gavilán, Jorge, 123-5

Tarragona, Julio, 128

Tellez, Antonio, 1

Tigre River, 88

Togliatti, Palmiro, 137*n*

trade unions, non-aligned, 72; Bakers, 22; drivers, 51, 126; Maritime, 9, 117

Tragedy in Dedham, 59

Tragic week, 1919 pogrom, 4, 16-17, *28n; 38*, 41, 49

Treni, Hugo, 57

Tribuna Proletaria, 29

Triple A commandos, Peronist, 130

Trotsky, L., 36

Twain, Mark, 91

U

University City, Madrid, 61

Uriburu, J.F.: coup of, 139; regime, 28n, 101-2, 111, 114-15, 122-3

Uriondo, Emilio, 80, 82, 85-6, 97, 101, 112, 116, 119-20, 128

Uruguay, 88, 93: police of, 93; Radical Colorado Party, 106-7; US Embassy bombing, 82, 85, 97

USA, Uruguay Embassy bombing, 82, 85, 97

Ushuaia, penal servitude location, 41, 44, 55, 77, 86, 113, 116, 129

V

Vanzetti, Bartolomeo, 59, 136-7

Varela, Colonel, 44n; killings by and killing of, 18, 85

Varela, Policeman, 42

Vasena workshops massacre, 28

Vázquez, Sotero F., 43

Vázquez Paredes, Andrés,
     79, 84-5, 87, 89, 93-
     4, 105, 110, 112, 119,
     131; 'disapeared', 133;
     presumed murder of, 132
Victor Emmanuel III, 136
Videla, J.R., dictatorship,
     133
Viedma prisoners, 56, 73;
     campaign for, 59
Viega, Manuel, 56
Vieytes asylum, 45
Voline, 1

W

Wilckens, Kurt, 44-5, 85;
     Varela assassination, 18
Wladimirovich, Boris, 34-6,
     38-45

Y

Yrigoyen, Hipólito, regime
     of; 28, 40-1, 49, 88, 102,
     111; overthrow of, 114

Z

Zavala, policeman, 93

Support **AK Press!**

AK Press is one of the world's largest and most productive anarchist publishing houses. We're entirely worker-run

& democratically managed. We operate without a corporate structure—no boss, no managers, no bullshit. We publish close to twenty books every year, and distribute thousands of other titles published by other like-minded independent presses from around the globe.

The Friends of AK program is a way that you can directly contribute to the continued existence of AK Press, and ensure that we're able to keep publishing great books just like this one! Friends pay $25 a month directly into our publishing account ($30 for Canada, $35 for international), and receive a copy of every book AK Press publishes for the duration of their membership! Friends also receive a discount on anything they order from our website or buy at a table: 50% on AK titles, and 20% on everything else. We've also added a new Friends of AK ebook program: $15 a month gets you an electronic copy of every book we publish for the duration of your membership. Combine it with a print subscription, too!

There's great stuff in the works—so sign up now to become a Friend of AK Press, and let the presses roll!

Won't you be our friend? Email friendsofak@akpress.org for more info, or visit the Friends of AK Press website: www.akpress.org/programs/friendsofak